THE SELF-MULTIPLICATION PRINCIPLE

Adapted from a talk given by
Walter Russell in 1946

University of Science and Philosophy
Swannanoa
Waynesboro, Virginia 22980
1993

The Self-Multiplication Principle

By Walter Russell

(1871 - 1963

Printed in the United States of America

ISBN 1-879605-39-2

Edited by Emilia Lee Lombardi
Printed by Mid Valley Press

We are fully aware of the

step-up transformer principle

in relation to the multiplication of

electric energy

but

few of us are aware of the

mental *step-up transformer principle*

which makes leaders of men

rather than followers.

THE SELF-MULTIPLICATION PRINCIPLE

"Think not thou of doing great works in my name. Go thou to thy neighbor. Think thou of thy neighbor alone. One seed sufficeth not for a meadow but out of one seed cometh a sheaf of ten."

Message of The Divine Iliad

The entirety of this message is for the uplift of man to a higher stage of his evolving. As I have told you many times, man progresses in cycles of approximately twenty-five hundred years. Messengers appear at the beginning of these cycles to bring new knowledge to man. These messengers are prepared by God with that knowledge by being taken behind the scenes, behind the illusions of matter in the universe, for the purpose of uplifting man one notch higher. This one notch higher is a dangerous period in man's evolution. He is threatened with self-destruction because of his having advanced too far into the sensed side of life and not sufficiently far into the spiritual side.

A tremendous spiritual awakening is due here now. This new age and this spiritual awakening must be based upon a greater comprehension of man, of his universe, and of his relation to God so that he may recollect more of his inheritance than he has ever known, and make use of it concentratively in order to offset the seeds of fear, hatred, greed, selfishness, empire-building, and all the old order of things that we still have. Therefore every man should have power—and that is the subject for tonight: POWER.

But, first, I always like to give you a few little gems from *The Divine Iliad* which is the direct word of God given to you through me:

"When man thinketh of body of man alone, denying Me in him, then is man's image man's, not Mine and man's, for the pattern of My rhythmic balanced image within man may not be seen by him; nor may the glory of My Light be seen in him, nor known by him

"When man thinketh Me, through knowing Me, then is he patterned by My image, and I am he.

"When man so thinketh, then may My balanced rhythmic image be seen in him, then, also, may the glory of My Light be seen in him and be known by him.

"When man so thinketh, then is man's Balance absolute.

"When man so thinketh, then hath he all power that I, thy Father-Mother, Thinker of Creation, hath.

"Seek ye, therefore, what ye will in Me and ye shall find it.

"Desire what ye will and, behold, it standeth before thee. Throughout the aeons it has been thine without thy knowing, e'en though thou hast but just asked for it.

"Sit thou not and ask, acting not, for unless thou reach out for thy desire, it shall not walk thy way to thee unaided by thy strong arms.

"Behold, I am within all things, centering them. And I am without all things controlling them, but I am not those things which I center and control.

"Behold in Me the fulcrum of My changing universe which but manifests change, though I change not, nor move.

"For I am Rest. In Me alone is Balance.

"He who would find power must know that he extends from Rest in Me and I am he.

"He who would find Rest must return to Me, be Me, be fulcrum of his own power."

From: *The Divine Iliad*

In those words is the secret of every man's power. It is the secret of my power. Ask what ye will and ye will receive; desire what ye will and you will receive. *"But sit ye not and ask, acting not, for thy desire will not come to thee unaided by thine own strong arms."*

Work Must Be Performed to Express Power

One must desire and then work, and not wish and affirm and say, "God will do it all; I won't do anything; I don't need to." God does not unfold the oak from the seed without the electric interchange of the two sides of the sun and the earth. *Work must be performed in order to express power*, but the power that we express is not in the body. The power that we express is in the still fulcrum of God centering every man—the one Light of God which centers everyone and every creating thing. In that still fulcrum of rest is all the power. The action which extends from it is the *expression of power,* and that is what we mean by Creation.

There is in this universe only Creator and Creation. Creation extends as two lights from the one still Light, just as two children on a seesaw—which extends from the still fulcrum from which they borrow their power—express creative action from that still fulcrum of Light.

Many, many people ask me to explain the secret of power which I have expressed *through action* in my life. It is not easy. I know the long, long years of planning to be what I am. I know the action and the work of any man who has achieved—such as a Paderewski or an Edison—the long, long years of expressing *through action* the inspiration that they draw from the Source of all things which centers them in the Spirit. But to explain that is not so easy.

Accumulate Power in Yourself

A man in one of our great business concerns, one day, asked me to tell him what was the matter with him. Why was it that life was so casual and so superficial? Why was it that he, who occupied a fine position and received a fine salary, was not the kind of man he would like to be?

"That's a very simple question to answer," I said. "You give concentrated attention year after year to a machine that you are working upon, a marvelous machine, hours and hours a day, until you have gotten that machine to do marvelous things. It sells for a lot of money. It is almost human. Perhaps it is more than human in its accuracy, in its ability to tabulate all sorts of things. The census that used to take so many years to get a report on can now be summed up by that machine in a few weeks. (He was one of the principal workers on it.) But you don't give that concentrated attention to yourself. You, who are manifesting God's Intelligence, are putting it all into the machine and neglecting to put any of it in yourself. Your personality is a 'wise-cracking' personality. Everybody likes you, yes, but you are superficial. There is no depth to you. You like jazz and dancing. You don't care for symphony, you say. You don't care for fine literature. You have made yourself into that kind of man, and you know it. *You have never accumulated power in yourself.*"

Now, the difference between that man and every great man that I have ever known is that the great man pays great attention to the design of himself instead of a machine. He gives concentrated attention to himself and to the perfection of every detail of the Spirit-man in him.

How Nature Multiplies Its Power

Let me tell you how Nature multiplies its power, and perhaps you will then better understand how man can multiply his power indefinitely. You will also understand, then, how I multiply my power as many times as I choose. Our friend, Glenn Clark,* said I have lived five lives in one. I have been known as the most versatile man in America, and such names as that, simply because of what I am going to explain to you tonight, *and you can do exactly the same thing for yourself.*

**The Man Who Tapped The Secrets Of The Universe* by Glenn Clark. University of Science and Philosophy, Swannanoa, Waynesboro, Virginia., 22980

Every man can multiply himself indefinitely if he follows the principles laid down by Nature. This is an electric universe and every expression of action, or motion, in it is an electric expression. And every one of them is either a dissipating expression or an accumulating one. You accumulate power or dissipate it in every single action in Nature.

The step-up transformer that the electrical laboratory uses is a very good example. You take an electric wire and string it along straight for ten miles, then pass a current of electricity through that wire and in every foot or so along that wire something is happening in the invisible universe around it, which you cannot see but you can *know*. You can take a magnet and hold it near that wire and by tests that you can make, you will find that there are little loops of electric current going around the wire at intervals. The scientists call them "loops of force"; and all along that ten miles of wire the current is the same and remains the same. It does not change by dissipation or accumulation until you curve it. The minute you curve it, and you curve those miles of wire into circles. then those loops of force are no longer parallel with each other. They are radial. The outer part of the loop of force is farther away from its center than the inner part because radially they come together at a point the moment you make that turn in the wire.

Now, the more turns you make in that wire, and the more electricity that has to go around and around and around the coils of wire, the more those loops of force come together and multiply the power of that current. So that same wire that had a current of power running through it of nominal voltage, when those loops of force are coiled and concentrated toward one common center they multiply that voltage hundreds or even thousands of times. That is what we call "stepping up" energy.

Nature does exactly the same thing. God winds up the electric current around a still point of Omnipresent Light which we call the center of gravity. God desires to extend His idea from the One Light into expression in two, so He winds the "electric coils" around and around and around the still point and produces a sun, an earth, a solar system. Instead of being coils of wire they are spheres, but it is the same thing. It is light, light concentrated in the direction of the still center and dissipated in the other direction.

Now, let us go back to the coil of wire. We have made, say, one hundred turns in that coil of wire. Let's make a thousand turns in it. We have multiplied it again. Let us make ten thousand turns in it. Now all those loops of force meet together in the middle, and there is an incandescent light there, an incandescent light and heat and concentrated electric power that is absolutely motionless at the center, forceful and positive as it gathers toward the center, and dissipated as it goes away from the center. The center of gravity in our earth is a good example. Our sun is a good example. That is what Nature does.

All The Power That Man Has Is In His Knowing

Now what does man do? The still center of man is the Kingdom of God, the still Light. And around that still Light is the coil, or a series of coils that we call "man," his knowing and thinking. There is no expression of power there, whatsoever, other than the power expressed in matter itself *until man knows and thinks. All the power that man has is in his knowing. And all of it is expressed only by his thinking.*

Now man is manifesting God on earth and he wishes to manifest Him with power, creative power and creative expression. So if man gives the attention to himself that the inventor I just spoke to you about gives to the machine that he is inventing, and if he is aware of the Source of power centering him and of God from whom he draws all power then he, himself, multiplies himself in exactly the same way that Nature does. The more concentrated the "coils" of his thinking are in expressing his knowing, the more power he has to express it and the more *awareness he has in him of the Source of power that he is expressing.*

Let us go into a day of work and see why a weakness, a dissipation of power, may be there, or an accumulation of it according to what we have done during the day.

To me the night is sacred. All my life I have summed up my day and asked myself what I have done during the day that multiplied my power or dissipated it. It might be a word spoken unkindly about a friend, someone's feelings hurt, an unwise action of my own, or neglect of an opportunity not taken. I would take a careful check of the entire day just as a machinist or an inventor would take check of his machine so that the next day that he worked upon the machine it would be so much better.

So I always check up on my day before I enter the sacred portals of night. Then I enter the sacred portals of night with the desire written upon my heart, written into the pulse-beat of the universe, as to what my next day should be. I ask and I desire the answer in my consciousness in the night, and it always comes. I would always have the answer. And the next day, in the morning, I did exactly the same thing before entering the sacred portals of the day, and recollected the answers to the questions I had asked of God during the night, and envisioned them, and had a half hour or an hour or more of intense ecstasy in that communion which made things so clear that were not clear the night before. It corrected the mistakes of the day before, making every defeat a stepping stone to a success for the day rather than to a defeat or to a loss or dissipation of power or energy. Then all day I worked at whatever it was, sculpting or painting or whatever task was set before me that I had chosen to do. I worked with full awareness and realization of the Kingdom of God around which I had wound the "coils" of desire and pulled them tighter. They were multiplied in the direction of the center.

Fix Your Eyes Upon The Heavens

Concentrated energy flowed toward the center —the center of Light, the center of Power— and it remained there so long as my eyes were fixed upon the heavens, so long as the eyes of the Spirit worked with the eyes of the body in creating my sculptural works, God with me, working with me, companion with me. Hours went by like minutes, intense joy in that feeling of multiplying power. And whenever I have been in that mood, knowing God in me, everything I did was a masterpiece. It couldn't be otherwise. But if I worked unknowingly, losing for a moment that ecstasy, being careless or casual, I knew that what I was doing at the time was not enduring, and I would wipe out hours of work, go to the door, symbolically kick Walter Russell out and let God in again.

Or I might sit at the piano for five minutes and find inspiration that way. And God would come back again, and the "coils" would tighten, the electric current would concentrate more and more.

Our dealings with our fellow men are a part of our life, of everybody's life. Whatever we do with respect to our neighbor, if it is not in harmony with that ecstasy of feeling that is within us, it will hold down our work, it will destroy whatever one is doing and it will be impossible to bring it back until one restores one's harmony and balanced feeling with respect to it, even in little things.

A salesman once said to me, "Goodness sake, I haven't had any sales today. I'm going out and sell that 'old gink' a bill of goods."

"You had better not go," I advised. "You will not sell him."

"Why?"

"You have destroyed all that makes it possible for you to make that sale through the very expression that you have just made, 'that old gink'. You are going to perform an action which is manifesting your Creator. It is an action benefitting you; it has to benefit him, too. It cannot benefit you or him *unless you and he are one.* You must know what he wants. You must then give him the thing that he requires and you must get the sale all signed on the dotted line before you leave here. You can only do that by making all of the elements of that sale right before you start. And a prime essential in one of those elements is to love that man that you are dealing with. He is part of your transaction. If I painted a picture with the attitude that you have in going to make that sale, it wouldn't be much of a picture. And your sale will not be much of a sale. You will not make it. You had better not go."

He said, "You know, Russell, I think you've got something there."

And he was serious because I had talked to groups of salesmen for such a long time. He thanked me for the criticism, saying:

"That was a good thing pulling me up like that. Now let's get together, shall we? How do I get into this right attitude?"

And when he had gotten into the right attitude, as I made it clear to him, he went out and made the sale. He could do it <u>then</u> because he had concentrated his power to a center, and then released it logically. And the logical thing had to happen. The effect always must follow the cause, and any idea that a man has, if it is set up properly as to cause, will consummate properly as to effect of cause.

An Example in Nature
Power Under Control

Let me illustrate by an example in Nature. One chemist, for example, might accumulate a tremendous volume of gasses and elements into a small package the size of an acorn. We'll call that a bullet. That is power multiplied in exactly the same way as the step-up transformer multiplies electric power—a large volume of space collected into a small volume of space; taken from the condition of rest and expansion and put into a condition of fast motion and contraction within a small space, and enclosed in a proper tube with a little cap that can be exploded.

Now, then, the trigger is pulled, the cap explodes, and all of that immense volume that has been accumulated and put into that little "bullet" explodes and dissipates into space in a fraction of a second. We call that an explosion. Well, ninety-nine out of a hundred people do just that thing most of the time, carefully and painstakingly accumulating one thing after another, accumulating power from time and space and distances and elements into a small package, and then by some unwise act, some act of intolerance, impatience, dishonesty, or unfair dealings with one's neighbor, explode it all at once. Gone!

Let's take another example: A tremendous volume again is concentrated into a little package, but this time it is an acorn, the size of a bullet but it is an acorn. *Now there is power under control.* It cannot possibly be exploded by a cap. It is put into the ground and slowly it unfolds its patterns. The manifestation of its purpose unfolds unto the heavens, and for one hundred years it grows, grows, grows into the manifestation of one of the ideas of God. It comes into being and unfolds its power. We call that growth. There is no difference, whatsoever, between the explosion of the bullet and the growth of the acorn except in time. A series of explosions—the one explosion divided into many but explosions just the same. A hundred-year explosion under control instead of a one-second explosion not under control.

Every Person Has To Know Himself.

Now, every person has to be absolutely under control, and the only way he can be under control is to know himself, know the Source of himself, and be *one* with the Source of himself. He has to have all the qualities of the Source of himself and draw upon those qualities for power and knowledge, and truth and law and balance, and the orderliness of every procedure in Nature.

Then he unfolds in the orderliness of that procedure *under control*—unfolds with love, balance, tolerance, and lack of any ill feeling in one's heart which would make it impossible for one to say a thing against one's neighbor.

Love in one's heart for one's work is manifesting God; pride for worthiness to be able to manifest God. Those are the things that men should do to accumulate power and energy by constantly multiplying those "coils" around that central Kingdom of God within one.

One night in New York, Dr. Clark was asked to pray in Calvary Church. And he recited the Lord's Prayer. *"Our Father, who art in heaven, hallowed be thy name, thy kingdom come. . ."* I stopped there; he went on. I most always stop there because I know what that means. I wish you knew what it means as I do. Jesus, when he said that, did not say it for the people of his day; he said it for the people who were to come that would know what he meant more than the people of his day. The Kingdom is the Light, and all mankind is searching for the Light, and eventually all mankind will find the Light. And that prayer simply means ". . . come the day when all men will know the Kingdom of God within them."

That day is two or three thousand years or so nearer to the goal. There are thousands and thousands of people now with more of an awareness of that Light in them, the Light of the Kingdom. And the more they are aware of the Light of the Kingdom in them, the more they can concentrate their power toward it and multiply the "coils" of their thinking—which is an expression of their knowing—and surround themselves with such a dynamo of power that they are creations of God's creations and are insulated from everything that should not touch them. That power insulates one from that which should be shut out.

I can walk through the ugliest of slums and see beauty. Think of the beauty that a Beethoven or Wagner or Rachmaninoff sees with the eyes of the Spirit and hears through the ears of the Spirit as he gets moods and rhythms from the chirping of insects or just the mood of the moon, or haze, or sometimes even of flowing rivers or streams. They hear those rhythms with the ears of the body, and they reinterpret them with the ears of the Spirit into inspired messages from the holy of holies within them.

Everything a Man Does Should Enrich the Whole Human Race

The power that they have multiplied within themselves, they give out. To multiply one's power one must divide that power, divide it and radiate it and give it out to the whole world. *For everything that man does to manifest God should enrich the whole human race.* And if at any time one seriously considers that proposition he should ask himself, "Am I at this moment doing something that will enrich the whole race?" Just as one drop of water raises the whole ocean, so does one beautiful thought from anybody uplift the whole race.

Rachmaninoff divides himself and gives himself to the whole of humanity for its uplift, and by so doing he multiplies himself by that "coil" coming ever tighter, ever tighter, ever, ever stepping up the transformer of power; ever, ever insulating himself from the dissipation of power, ever safeguarding himself from outside influences until he can forget his body and live wholly in the inspiration of communion between himself and his centering God.

That is my answer to you as to how I have multiplied my powers. *You can do what I have done.* Everyone can do what I have done by thinking what you know into creative expression and multiplying your thinking and your knowing by your awareness of God centering you, and realizing the holiness of it and of your wonderful opportunity in life to manifest the Creator. There is nothing in the world greater that a man can do. And to be worthy of doing it should be the greatest ambition of every man.

I give these thoughts for your consideration. I sincerely trust you will give deep consideration to them for the multiplication of power by awareness of the Light within you, by being fulcrum of your own power, by using that fulcrum of the Kingdom of God within you for your own expression of power.

A THOUGHT TO REMEMBER

This is but a thought universe, an electric record of the thinking of Mind. The reality of you is not in your body. The only interest you should have in your body is the mental interest in building it into the kind of body you would like it to be to manifest you. You build your own body in the image of your Self.

Whatever your Self is, your body will be. Whatever your thoughts are, your body will record, whether balanced or unbalanced, good or bad, sickness or health, misery or supreme happiness. The eternal you is a glorious illumined, divine being. Do you know your Self as that? To the extent that you do know your Self

as a glorious, transcendent being, your body will manifest that glory in every cell of it. It cannot help doing so. Electric recordings of thoughts in matter are automatic. It is Law. It never errs.

Forget your body, therefore. Your body will automatically be what your thoughts are. Build a beautiful, healthful, sound, vital body by thinking transcendent thoughts and putting those thoughts into action for the good of your neighbor and the world. Put Mind first, body last. Live in an ecstatic mental reality and make your body conform to the balanced rhythms of ecstasy.

Remember this—never for a moment forget it—that Mind controls motion and desire of Mind furnishes the power to motivate motion. The troubles of man arise from the fact that matter and motion control him. His inability to recognize the fact that the sensations caused by the motion of matter will dominate him and lead him toward a selfish, greedy life of seeking unreal possessions whereas a mental existence will dominate those sensations to his everlasting glory.

No matter how little any man has to give, it
will return
to him multiplied unto his own glory.
That is the Law.

You must work knowingly with
God knowing that God is working with
you--giving you exactly what you are
able to give back equally from
moment to moment and not more,
but
setting no limitations on what He will give.
God lets you set those limitations
which may be bounded or unbounded,
or be as great or small as your desire is
great or small.

"There are those among men of earth who deem desire unholy. These seek holiness, and Me, through the suppression of all desire.

"These sit in quietude, seeking me through meditation, but acting not to manifest My purpose. Yet these ask alms, in My name, of those who fulfill My purpose through thought followed by action.

"I command thee to tell to these misguided holy men, who sell their holiness for a price to those who unknowingly buy naught of holiness for their wasted gold, that they who thus sit begging by the road in mortifying rags shall never find Me, whom they seek, until they act to fulfill my purpose."

From: *The Divine Iliad*

TIG'S

The street was strangely quiet. Footsteps were muffled in the fog. Shoes slipped and slithered on the wet pavements. Voices were hushed; an occasional laugh, a muttered curse, nothing more.

It was by the street lamp that Bill realised he was not alone. He'd heard nothing, he could see nothing, but some inner sense told him that there were people round him, closing in and squeezing him.

A voice, whispering and low, cut through the darkness.

'Bill! Money for the Badden, Bill. We've come to get the money.'

'No! Get away from me! You'll not have it!'

He tried to swing his arm round to clear the way before him, but there was nothing there to hit. The same chanting voices pressed nearer to him.

'We've come to get the money, Bill. Money for the Badden.'

He opened his mouth to shout, but no sound came. He stood stock-still in the darkness, waiting . . .

More mystery and adventure in Lions

Twisters *Steve Bowles*
Grimm Grange *William Browning*
Spellbinders in Suspense *Alfred Hitchcock*
Cold River *William Judson*
The Third Class Genie *Robert Leeson*
Master of Morgana *Allan Campbell McLean*
The Hill of the Red Fox *Allan Campbell McLean*
My Mate Shofiq *Jan Needle*
Z For Zachariah *Robert O'Brien*
Through a Brief Darkness *Richard Peck*
The Undertaker's Gone Bananas *Paul Zindel*

Tig's Crime

T. R. BURCH

FONTANA · LIONS

First published 1979
by William Heinemann Ltd.
First published in Lions February 1981
by William Collins Sons & Co Ltd
14 St James's Place, London sw1

Printed in Great Britain by
Richard Clay (The Chaucer Press) Ltd,
Bungay, Suffolk

One

PATCHES of fog rolled along the street like puffs of smoke from a kettle. It crept into doorways and through gaps in the railings by the Baptist Church. As they passed, cars and buses whisked it away for a moment, but the clear space, lit intermittently by the orange lamps high overhead, was filled again before a man could safely cross the road. The big department store opposite, its windows flashily decorated for Christmas two months in advance, came and went like a great ship lurching through a choppy sea.

Old Bill sat in his little wooden hut crammed into the corner between the White Lion Hotel and the police station. It was cold, as well as foggy. But Bill never shivered. He had often wondered, when other people stood in front of him with their fingers shaking so much they could hardly fish the coppers out of their pockets, why he should be spared this affliction. He *felt* the cold, yes. But he never shivered. Perhaps it was something to do with the way his rum old body was made. There had to be some compensations.

A hunched figure shambled through the mist into the pool of light shed by the lamp Bill always kept hanging from the roof.

"*Evening Herald.*"

Bill passed him the paper, took the money, said, "Thank you, sir," cheerfully, as he always did, this time maybe with a shade more emphasis to make up for his customer's lack of civility. The figure disappeared into the gloom, his back no more communicative than his face.

A few more customers emerged from the fog, bought their papers, passed on. Some he knew, his regulars. Some had a few words for him, mostly about the weather. Some were joylessly cheerful, others silent as the grave. He'd be glad when it was time to pack up and go.

He glanced up at the illuminated clock on the church wall. A great round moon-face, blearily dim, the hands just visible. Another hour yet.

A policeman sauntered down the steps of the police station, looked up and down the street, came over to Bill's wooden hut. The lamplight twinkled on the metal of his uniform. Bill looked at him with mild interest. It wasn't often you saw a policeman on foot nowadays.

"Nice evening," he said, with no particular emphasis.

"Seen worse."

"Paper?"

"No thanks. Got the beat to do."

"That's new, isn't it? You back on your feet, like?"

"It does come a bit strange. But orders from above, *you* know. Cars are all very well for the motorways, and the big time stuff, and that. But they start young nowadays. Little things — a pencil or two from Woolworths, an apple off a market stall. And they don't get caught, so they go on. And they're doing an empty house or knocking down some solitary tramp before they're the age to vote. They're all right by themselves, but it's when they get together, that's where the trouble starts. And you don't know what they're up to half the time. You know what my boy told me the other day?"

"No?"

"Eleven, he is. A good lad. Does well at school. But he had a bit of a cold, and he was coughing pretty fierce the other evening, so I said to him, as a joke, you see, 'Trouble with you, my lad,' I says, 'is you smoke too much.' And you know what he said?"

"What?"

"Looks me straight in the eye, and says he only has ten a day. I ask you! Bit of a shock that was. I asked him where he got the money from, but I couldn't get much sense out of him. Evasive. Must be losing my touch. I can usually get 'em to squeal."

The policeman chuckled at his own failings. Bill watched him silently.

"You after anyone now, then?" he said.

"Not so's you'd notice. These kids!"

The policeman looked along the road again, pushed his shoulders back, and sighed.

"Cheerio, pop. Look out for the villains, and don't take any wooden shillings." He strolled away.

Bill watched him disappear into the mist.

It was strangely quiet in the street. Footsteps were muffled in the fog-laden atmosphere. Shoes slipped and slithered on the wet pavements, made treacherous by fallen leaves. Voices were hushed, almost as though their owners were afraid to break the circle of dim light in which they moved. The scent of a cigarette hung in the air long after the smoker had thrown away the stub and gone. Even the queue of people waiting patiently for seats in the cinema opposite was still. An occasional laugh, a muttered curse as someone nearly walked into a parking meter, nothing more.

A small red-haired head appeared suddenly over the top of the wooden counter. It was a girl's face with a mass of freckles, mostly hidden by splashes of mud.

"Got the time?"

Old Bill shifted slightly on the high bench that served him as a chair.

"It's up there, on the church clock," he said. "Nearly half-past six."

The little figure with the red hair grunted. "Got a light, mister?"

"You're too young to smoke."

"Nah! It's for a firework. See?"

Old Bill shook an admonitory finger.

"Don't you go setting them things off here. Mind, now. It ain't allowed in the street."

"All right then." The voice betrayed no particular emotion. "Got a penny for the guy?"

"Where's the guy, then?"

"Round the back, down the alley."

"I'd have to see it first, whether it was worth a penny."

"Go on."

"No!" Old Bill was suddenly firm. "Clear off!"

The figure paid no attention. One dirty hand crept over the edge of the counter.

"You've got plenty of money there. You wouldn't miss a penny or two. Just a penny for the guy."

"Ain't my money. I have to hand it in."

"They wouldn't miss it. Just a penny for the guy." The voice took on a beggar's whining sing-song chant, half real, half self-mocking.

Old Bill took a penny out of his pocket. "There you are. Now, go on, clear off!"

The red-haired figure offered no word of gratitude, but grabbed the penny and made off down the alley at the back of the hut.

"Kids!" Old Bill muttered to himself. You couldn't do a thing with 'em, these days, or *to* them either. In any case, they were always so much bigger than he was. Even though the police station was only just across the alley, it seemed remote and unhelpful. Old Bill wasn't prepared to argue the toss with any bunch of layabout kids.

Nearly time now. A few more minutes, and he could pack up and go. He would put all the money, as usual, apart from his float, in the flat leather bag which the firm gave him; then pull down the shutters on the shed (that always cost him a bit of an effort); out at the back, lock up, down the alley. On the way home he would put the bag of money through the letterbox of the *Evening Herald* office. That was down at the end of the alley, and it was generally pretty dark, the way Bill liked it. Nobody saw him, or knew what he was about. He always kept right up against the wall, out of sight. It saved a lot of bother. You had to be careful, when you were less than four feet high. Some people laughed at him, and he had grown used to that. It was the quick turning away of the head which indicated that someone didn't *want* to see him. That was what upset him, even after all these years. Well, he was hardly likely to grow much more now. Not at seventy.

Time to go. He waited just a few more minutes to see if any late-comers might want a paper, but the street was deserted, dank, and forlorn. Even the dejected cinema queue had shuffled into the warmth of the lobby. Glad to be out of the cold, whatever the film was, Bill thought. And it was *cold*. Freezing fog they talked about on the weather forecast. The cold seemed to seep right into him. But he never shivered.

He emerged through the door at the back, a little man, his pocket heavy and distended with the flat bag in which he kept the money. The fog clung round him like a protecting blanket. He was glad of it: nobody would notice him in this lot.

He locked the hut door, and moved into the deeper blackness of the alley. His little feet made hardly a sound on the wet tarmac. He knew the way without looking. Something brushed against his leg, but he knew what it was. The cat that roamed the alley all day and night was out looking for his supper.

There should have been a street lamp half-way down the alley, but someone had thrown a stone at it a few nights ago. Broken bits of plastic still lay scattered about the foot of the column, but no one had thought to report it to the proper authorities, or if they had, no one had come to mend it. Not that it mattered. Old Bill knew every inch of his way without a light.

It was by the street lamp that he realised he was not alone. He had heard nothing, and he could see nothing, but some inner sense told him that there were people round him, closing in and squeezing him, though there was nothing to feel and nothing to fight against. Was it that he could *smell* them?

A voice, whispering and low, cut through the darkness.

"Bill! Money for the Badden, Bill. We've come to get the money, Bill. We've come . . ."

"No!" Bill roared. "Get away from me! You'll not have it!"

He tried to swing his arm round to clear the way before him, but there was nothing there to hit. The same quiet chanting voices pressed nearer to him.

"We've come to get the money, Bill. Money for the Badden."

He opened his mouth to shout, but no sound came. He stood stock-still in the darkness, waiting. Just waiting. He felt himself shiver, just once, but a lump of wood came down on his head, and he dropped to the ground. He didn't shiver any more.

Two

TIG stood in the queue patiently waiting for the cinema to have seats available. He had just enough money for the cheapest seats, and he jingled the coins in his pocket to help keep his spirits up. It was cold and damp, and the fog clung round him. The hair of the man in front of him shone with moisture.

Tig looked up and down the street as far as his eyes could penetrate the soft oozing blanket. The only sign of warmth came from the illuminated signs above the cinema door. He had made for this beacon because he was lonely and miserable. He knew it was an X-film, but he hoped they'd take pity on him and let him in. Perhaps if he stood on his toes when he got to the paybox? He tried standing on his toes, but it didn't seem to make much difference: the man in front with his arm round his girlfriend, still towered over him. He tried to remember what he looked like, but he had never spent much time looking in the mirror, and it came to him as a bit of a shock that he might easily fail to recognise himself if he met himself coming down the road . . . The thought amused him for a moment, and he grinned. His eyes glowed in the light from the cinema, and his snub nose looked red from laughter rather than cold.

Tig's mind turned idly back to the events of the day. He supposed he ought to be worried or something, but he wasn't. He hadn't been home since eight this morning, and he didn't much care whether he ever went home again. He'd been in trouble before he left for school — his shirt was muddy. Well, what if it was? Smithy and he had had a bit of an argument on the way back from school the day before. It was over the common, which in this sort of weather was mucky and treacherous, and he had fallen in a shallow puddle after one of Smithy's wild blows happened to land on his nose. Tig rubbed his nose reflectively. It was still a bit sore. Smithy packed a good punch. They had enjoyed that argument.

So there was mud on his collar. His mother had moaned at him. The words were always the same. "If your Dad was here, you'd get what for." Tig knew she had a hard time of it. It was years now since his father had been home: he could just remember him, but it was an effort. He wondered if he ever really *wanted* to see him again. Perhaps, one day, when he was big enough to stand up for himself . . .

That was always the trouble. Too small, they said, when he tried to push himself forward in anything at school. Not big enough. Wait a year or two, boy. You'll grow. Well, he couldn't help being small. He wasn't a midget, anyway . . .

'Okkerd' Oakham addressed him as 'little man', and though Tig knew it was meant to be friendly, he was not too sure the other kids in the class took it that way. There was just a hint of 'teacher's pet' in it, and that, at Hill Lane Comprehensive, was the worst thing you could say about anybody. Tig shivered as the cold fog bit into his thin frame. A slow grin spread over his button features. He was remembering the firework . . .

It had started early in the day. When Mr Oakham came in to take the register, there had been a bit of a fight going on at the back. Nothing much, but noisy. It had taken Okkerd a few minutes to sort things out, and in the process somebody swore at him. He hadn't known who it was. It might have been Tig, though in fact it wasn't. Okkerd thought it safest to pick on someone insignificant.

"English! You in the corner!"

Tig, hearing himself spoken to, hurriedly pulled himself together. His eyes widened. The only emotion he felt was a bitter resentment at the unfairness of it. He hadn't said a solitary word, not one. Just because he was small, that's all it was.

"English, you will report to me here in the break."

That probably meant detention.

And then at the beginning of break, Tig had found himself in possession of a firework. He wasn't certain how he had come by it. There had been a lot of people milling about in the playground; a game of football with a tennis-ball was going on, showing more energy than skill. And there he was, clutching a 'thundering volcano', the bang of the century. At least, that's what it said on the wrapper. 'Light blue touch-paper, and stand well clear.' Who had shoved it into his hand? The master on duty was standing at the door of the main block, looking grimly just over everybody's heads. Someone was trying to get rid of the evidence, just in case there was a search. Fireworks were strictly forbidden. So Tig now had one, a good big banger, in his trouser pocket.

He slouched away to the wall of the sports hall, and leant against its rough surface. It was then that an idea floated into his mind. Well, it was time he got a bit of his own back, wasn't it?

Tig changed his chewing-gum to the other side of his mouth. Of course, there were problems. How to get the banger under Okkerd Oakham's chair just at the right moment. With the blue touch-paper smouldering, too.

Tig ambled towards the door.

"What do you want, boy?"

"Got to see Mr Oakham, sir. He said so."

"All right." The master on duty stepped to one side and allowed Tig in. Tig climbed the broad stairs to the classroom. He knocked at the door.

"Come in."

Tig went in, and found Mr Oakham by himself, filling a

plastic mug from a thermos flask.

"You're late, English. I said the beginning of break."

"Sorry, sir. I got held up. Someone else wanted me. I couldn't get away." The lie was vague enough to be safe.

"Impertinence cannot be tolerated. You spoke rudely to me this morning."

"It wasn't me," Tig said.

"Don't interrupt. I know what I heard. I am convinced it was you. And mere denial will not serve your interests."

Tig looked at the floor and said nothing. He wasn't really listening, anyway. Mr Oakham went on for some minutes. Tig might not have bothered to hear any of it, except that one sentence leapt at him from the confused welter of words and hit him in the face.

"Of course," Mr Oakham said, "I realise that, with your family background, I can hardly expect any better from you."

Red anger burst into flame behind Tig's eyes. He went on looking at the floor, but his fists were clenched. 'Family background'. That meant his mother. Had old Okkerd been round to his home and talked to his mother? Cheek, that's what it was. Anger died away, leaving a cold and careful determination. Mr Oakham's voice flowed on.

The bell went. A pounding of feet on the bare stairs, large bodies crowding in through the door, girls swinging bags, boys with ties loose and muddy boots. Tig stood in the corner by the door, covered by the continuous traffic. He felt for the box of matches he always kept in his right-hand pocket.

Okkerd Oakham had asked for it.

Most of the class had now got to their places. A sort of quiet descended on the room.

"Sit down, English. Sit down, all of you."

Tig walked deliberately behind Mr Oakham's chair. The scrape of the match was covered by the assorted noises of books, pens, and shuffling shoes. Tig walked on to his place. Just as he sat down, the banger went off. The detonation, shatteringly loud in the enclosed room, was followed by three seconds' shocked silence. Tig smiled.

He was smiling now, as he thought of it, standing coldly in the cinema queue with the fog filling his lungs. It had been a moment worth waiting for.

Well, he'd got himself thrown out of the class, and he'd gone without regret, followed by a stream of threats. That didn't worry him. He'd walked straight out of the door, fished for a cigarette as he stood by the ornamental pond at the front of the school, and puffed happily away. He knew, without looking, that one of the teachers was watching him and was making for the door to come after him.

Tig waited for a few more seconds, flicked the spent match into the pond, and ambled down the road. At his own speed. He heard his name called, but he ignored it. They'd have to use force to get him back inside there again, and somehow he didn't think they'd use force.

He mooched through the town, looking at shop windows, for the rest of the day. It was when it was beginning to get dark, that he started to wonder what to do next.

Go home?

And face his mother?

What'd be the story this time? In any case, she had a knack of seeing through his stories. No, if he was going to be hanged, he might as well have a good evening first. He hadn't much money on him, but what he had was just enough for fish and chips and a film. Well, he'd had the fish and chips and with any luck they'd let him in to see the film.

He looked at the dim circle of the church clock. Fine, it was nearly time for the next house. The queue began to crawl towards the bright foyer of the cinema. Tig clutched his money. He *wanted* to see this film.

He came to the box-office, stood on his toes, lowered his voice. He should have known his luck wouldn't last. He tried pleading, but the bouncer at the door was moving in his direction, and a grey hopelessness settled on him.

He left the cinema lights, crossed the road, not bothering to look where he was going. He had in mind to go and see Pete. He might get a cup of tea at Pete's place. He entered the black alley behind the news-stand, his hands pushed deep in the pockets of his jeans, his shoulders hunched, his eyes on the ground. He saw nothing, he heard nothing.

Three

THE alley behind the news-stand was a tunnel of blackness. Tig knew his way though, and he wasn't bothered by the dark. There should have been a light half-way down, but there was no light to pierce the fog. Tig stumbled on, kicking at tin cans and old bottles.

Just by the lamp standard, where there should have been a pool of yellow light, but there wasn't, Tig looked up. He could hear the soft footfall of someone coming towards him. For some reason he could not understand, he didn't want to be seen. He knew he was out late, and he knew he was in trouble, and he wished to be left to himself. He put out a hand, found the lamp standard, and eased himself into the space between it and the wall. His foot scraped against some sort of obstacle, but he took no notice. His attention was focused on the approaching footsteps.

There was a pair of soft-sounding rubber soles, and another pair that clattered and clinked, creating the impression of high heels and steel tips. A little gleam of light glowed for a second in the middle of the road, and was gone. The footsteps ceased. Tig tried to hold his breath. A few muttered words come to his ears, but nothing that made sense.

Tig pressed his back against the roughness of the wall. It seemed more important than anything he could think of that he should not be seen. The words ceased, and the footsteps began again, soft and insistent, coming towards him.

A sort of panic gripped Tig's mind, and he wanted to run, but his muscles refused to move. The footsteps came nearer and nearer. A sudden thought flashed through Tig's consciousness: if he liked, he could put out a hand and *touch* them. That would make them jump. The footsteps stopped again, a few yards from him. Tig turned his head to catch the slightest sound. He could hear nothing, but a strange sweet smell came to his nostrils, like a woman's face-powder. In a moment it was gone, but for that moment the scent had a peculiarly lasting quality. Tig felt his nose tickling, and for one dreadful second he was afraid he was going to sneeze.

The light of a torch glowed again briefly. The owners of the footsteps seemed to have passed him, and now to be standing against the wall a matter of five yards from him.

There came the creak of a window opening. Another torch shone from higher up the wall. Tig tried to think what building it was of which this was the side wall. The police station? No, that was the other side of the alley. It must be the back of the White Lion Hotel.

A muttered curse brought Tig's attention back to the window. A square of dim light filtered through the fog. It was difficult to see, but Tig thought he could make out the outline of someone at the window, a fat outline, monstrously misshapen. Then as he watched, part of the outline detached itself and fell to the ground below with a soft thud. It sounded like a leather brief-case. The two shadowy figures at the foot of the wall gathered up the case. The square of light above them was extinguished, and a faint creak accompanied the shutting of the window. Complete silence.

Tig had almost ceased to breathe. He wanted to get away, he wanted to go home, but he knew that was no use. Had those two shadowy figures gone? He strained his ears to pick up any sound of footsteps.

A sudden blazing light dazzled his eyes, and he froze to the lamp standard. Surely they must see him? The beam of the torch travelled swiftly round in a narrow circle, stopping momentarily at the kerb and the line of the wall. It swung this way and that, and for a fraction of a second lit up the features of one of the figures. A broad nose, small dark eyes, a mass of black hair over the eyebrows, a beard.

And then, just as suddenly, the light had gone, leaving a darkness more impenetrable, more solid, more all-covering. The soft patter of footsteps faded away up the alley.

Tig expelled a gusty breath. He moved his hand up the lamp standard, and found a sort of comfort in its cold solidity. He squeezed himself out from the narrow gap. He trod carefully, remembering a dark shadow which had sprung into his sight as the torchbeam swung round. An old sack, or a squashed cardboard box, he thought, perhaps a dustbin on its side, though for one moment part of it had taken on the appearance of a face. He explored the pavement with a foot. The obstruction was soft and yielding. Tig knelt down cautiously: at all costs he must avoid making a noise. His hands moved to discover the edges of whatever it was that lay on the pavement in the blackness.

His fingers stiffened. With a gulp of terror he realised his hands had touched hair, wet and stiff, and a man's ear.

Tig got up slowly. There was no doubt in his mind now. There was nothing he could do for the body on the pavement. But he must get away. Pete. Pete would know what to do. Tig began to run, tripped, caught himself by the lamp standard, ran again. He had no thought for the noise his shoes made on the wet stones. He wanted to escape. He ran.

Pete's family lived in a terraced house a few streets away. There was a lane at the back of the terrace, serving a row of dilapidated sheds and garages. Tig burst through the back gate, stumbled among dustbins and stacks of secondhand tyres, up to Pete's back door. There was a light in the kitchen, where Pete was sitting at the table, with a paper of fish and chips in front of him. He was not surprised when Tig tumbled through the door.

"Have a chip?" Pete pushed the greasy paper a few inches across the table. Tig shook his head. He went to the sink, found a glass, and filled it from the tap.

The room, dim and dusty, was reassuring. Tig had spent a good many hours here, thinking it a second home. He had known Pete ever since they had both arrived at the same primary school on the same day years ago. Pete was one of the family; he could talk to Pete. The panic began to drain from his chest. He took a grip of the glass of water, working his fingers round its comforting firmness. He looked out of of the little window above the sink. He could see nothing but a dim square of light, misty and obscured, from the next-door house.

"There's a body in the alley by the police station."

His voice was flat and lacked all emotion.

Pete went on eating chips. The fingers of his left hand were busy with the slice of fish. His eyebrows rose a fraction, but he knew Tig better than to ask silly questions.

Tig, still looking out of the window, raised the glass to his mouth, and gulped down a long draught of cold, clear water. He put the glass down on the wooden draining-board, and turned slowly towards Pete, keeping his hands behind him.

"There's a man in the alley. He's dead."

Pete's hands stayed still on the table. He looked quickly up at Tig, recognised by his strained and ferocious face that this was no joke, and let his eyes fall to the pile of chips.

"I found him. 'Bout half-way down. You known that street light? It got broken a week ago. All dark. But I saw him on the pavement."

Tig's eyes were withdrawn and dark. His gaze, like Pete's, was fixed on the pile of chips, but he did not see them.

"He was dead."

"How do you know?" Pete's question was matter-of-fact.

"I felt his head. He wasn't breathing. There was blood all over his face."

Tig slowly withdrew his hands from behind him, splayed them out in front of Pete's face, showed him the dark brown stains.

"You'd better wash," said Pete, still matter-of-fact.

Tig turned quickly, grabbed a bar of soap, and began to scrub his fingers under a running tap.

"And your face."

Tig scraped at his face with uncaring fury.

"Here, hang about. You'll do yourself an injury."

Pete pulled himself up and hauled his long frame over to the sink. He dabbed at Tig's face with a wet cloth.

"You'll do. Who have you killed? Have a chip."

Tig sat at the table and looked at his hands. "The blood's gone," he said.

"I should hope so. You looked a mess. Who was he?"

"I don't know!" Tig sounded irritable. "It was just a head. All over blood. You couldn't see properly. There were these blokes."

"Blokes?"

"Yeah. Two of them. They had a torch."

"What were they doing?" Pete was interested.

Tig shrugged. "Dunno. Up to something funny. There was something that a man pushed out of the window high up in the wall. You know, the White Lion."

"Thieves?"

"Suppose so. The two at the bottom picked up whatever it was. They had a torch. I think they saw me. The light from the torch just flashed across the pavement. And there was this shape."

Tig stared in front of him at a brown picture of Southend Pier decorating the wall, but all he could see was the twisted white face streaked with something which might have been mud but wasn't.

Pete pushed his bag of chips over towards him. Tig shook his head angrily, but all the same helped himself. Pete followed his every move.

"Who killed him? Them two, you reckon?"

Tig thought. "No. They came along after. The bloke must have been there before. Not long, though. He was still warm."

Tig looked at the chip in his hand, and put it back in the bag.

"Pete, what am I going to do?"

"It's nothing to do with you, is it? I mean, you didn't kill him."

"But he was just lying there."

"Knocked over by a car, or maybe just slipped on the kerb. Pure accident."

Tig shivered. "You didn't see him. That was no accident."

"A car, then."

"You can't drive down there. There's that row of bollards at the end by the hut where they sell papers."

"Did you see anybody else?"

"No."

"You're in the clear, then. You sure nobody saw you?"

"Not unless it was the two blokes with the torch."

"You're laughing, then."

Tig got up, and went back to the sink. He looked out at the blackness of the dingy yard.

"I've got to tell someone," he said, trying to keep the desperation out of his voice. His hands gripped the edge of the sink.

"You have. Me."

Tig took no notice. "I can't just leave him there. I could phone the police. You know, without saying who I was."

"They won't let you. You'll have to give your name." Pete sounded as though he knew. Tig went on looking at the window-frame.

"Pete, I haven't been back home yet. I walked out of

school this morning."

"I know," said Pete. "Someone told me. They said you'd shot up old Okkerd. That right?"

"Only a firework."

Pete chuckled. Tig whipped round and glared at him, his mouth open to shout. Then he saw Pete, and heard Pete's careless laughter, and he was suddenly so angry that he could find nothing to say.

Tig slammed out of the back door, kicked into the dustbins and ran down the ash path to the gate which led to the lane. He didn't care what Pete said. He had to tell someone. And it would have to be the police.

Tig came out into the main street by another road. He couldn't face the thought of the dark alley and the body lying on the pavement in the fog. As he approached the police station, his steps slackened, and he had to force himself to push open the door which led to the counter.

It took him some time to persuade anyone to take any notice of him. And when he had persuaded them, and he led a reluctant constable down the black alley past the news-stand to the broken lamp standard, there was nothing there.

Four

TIG sat on a wooden chair in a corner of the reception hall at the police station. A few yards from him stretched a long dark counter, behind which stood a sergeant, busy with a large ledger and a battery of telephones. At the end of the room, high on the wall, was a clock with a cracked glass. It was nearly a quarter-past eight.

Tig stared at the floor, perfectly still, but his mind was a jumble of pictures which he was trying to sort out and put in order. That mud-streaked face had been *real.* The blood on his own hands had been real: the water, with which he had washed his hands, had turned red in the sink at Pete's place. It had really happened. Or had it? He pushed one hand through his spiky hair. The movement attracted the attention of the sergeant at the counter.

"Have you come round, then?" The sergeant's voice was roughly kind, but his eyes were puzzled. Funny little perisher, he thought, with his pinched white face and his hair sticking up in spikes. He looked bright enough, a pair of good sharp eyes on him. The sergeant had seen many examples of shock passing through this room, and he was pretty certain he could recognise the real thing when he saw it, and spot the sham and the play-acting, too. And this was real. He'd been talkative enough when he'd come bursting in with his silly story about a body in the alley. If he'd been older, you'd have put it down to alcohol. Perhaps that was it, after all. They started young nowadays.

The sergeant shifted his weight from one foot to the other, and went on with his work at the desk, keeping half an eye on Tig all the time. Shattered, he looked. Hadn't said a word since Sawyer brought him back. Well, somebody would have to find out where he came from sooner or later and take him home. It was a nasty night to be out by yourself. How old would he be, now? The sergeant sucked a pencil reflectively. Couldn't be much above twelve.

"You'll be about twelve, I suppose," he said.

Tig looked up, nettled. "Fourteen," he growled.

"Oh, you've got a tongue, then," the sergeant said comfortably. "I was beginning to wonder. Small for fourteen, aren't you?"

Tig said nothing. He'd heard that comment before, and he had given up worrying about it.

The sergeant sighed. He tried another opening.

"I could find you a cup of tea, if you like."

"Wouldn't mind."

The sergeant picked up a phone, flicked a switch, and ordered two cups of tea. "Sugar?" He cocked an eye at Tig. Tig nodded.

"Plenty of sugar," the sergeant said. He put down the phone. "You'll feel better after a nice cup of tea."

"I'm all right," Tig said irritably.

"Course you are."

A woman police officer entered with a tray. Tig took one of the two cups and drank thirstily. The sergeant watched him from under his heavy eyebrows.

"What was it you saw down that alley?"

"I told you."

"I know you told us what you thought you saw, but it wasn't there, was it?"

"I can't help it. It *was* there." Some of Tig's natural aggressiveness was returning to him as he drank the hot sweet tea.

"I'm going." He got up and made for the door.

"Not yet." The sergeant still sounded comfortable. "I've got to make a report, even if it is a whole lot of nonsense. Silly joke, really."

Tig glared. He felt a sudden gust of anger welling up inside him, and he wanted to get away, but he found that the sergeant's massive bulk was between him and the door. He stayed where he was.

"Calm down, son. Now, you just stand there, while I get a few facts down on paper." The sergeant moved back behind the desk.

"Now," he said. "Name?"

Tig snorted. So they thought they'd get him that way, did they? With a cup of tea and a fatherly manner. He'd have to give a false name and address, and then they'd let him go. He wracked his brains for a suitable name.

"French," he muttered.

The sergeant wrote it down at the top of a sheet of clean paper.

"French, eh?" he repeated. "You look English enough to me." He chuckled happily to himself: have to put the lad at his ease, he thought.

"French," Tig snapped, but then a grin broke over his thin face, and he laughed aloud. He was beginning to enjoy himself.

"That's better." The sergeant beamed. "Christian name?"

"John," said Tig, truthfully. There was no harm in telling them that, nobody had called him John for years.

"Right, John French. Address?"

"Six Lime Road." Tig found his lies coming easier.

The main doors swung open as the sergeant laboriously wrote down the address. Two patrolmen came in, bringing with them a broken-down old tramp, the worse for alcohol. The sergeant's attention was distracted and, with a brief "Hold on a minute, lad," he turned to the tramp.

"Joe Henderson, again," the sergeant said wearily.

"What is it this time?"

"Drunk in the gutter, just round the corner," one of the patrolmen reported.

"Where exactly?"

"Just past the news-stand. At the mouth of the alley."

The sergeant beamed at Tig, who still stood by the desk. "That explains it, son. This is the man you saw. Right?"

Tig looked at the tramp. His hair was matted, and it mingled with an unkempt beard which covered his neck. He had a dirty face and a red nose. But there was no blood.

"No," Tig said. He took his cup of tea and sat in the corner on the hard wooden chair. His head was steadier now, and events were clear in his mind. First, this wasn't the same face. Tig forced himself to bring to his eyes the picture as he remembered it. The lamp standard; the two thieves at the wall of the hotel; the dim circle of light sweeping round and falling for an instant on a pattern of black and grey. He shivered. No, it was not the same face. And another thing, the tramp had been found at the mouth of the alley, not half-way down it. He couldn't have been there long, either, or he would have seen him when he went back with the policeman to find the body. The body that wasn't there.

Tig shifted his feet and put down the cup. He stared at his shoes, making patterns on the tiled floor with his toes.

Perhaps he had imagined it. The police obviously didn't believe him. Pete had laughed at him. And anyway, did it matter? Pete had been right: it would have been better not to have got himself involved. John French! That had been a good idea. A slow grin spread over his face, a grin which stayed fixed and unreal.

He was looking at his shoes. He had been scraping his toes along the lines of the tiles. The toe-caps were splashed with dark stains, and something damp and sticky filled the thin gap between sole and upper. Tig remembered the feeling as his foot had struck against an obstacle, soft and yielding, in the blackness of the alley. He put down a hand to scratch at the dark stain, but he knew what it was.

Blood.

That proved he hadn't been dreaming. It was real. Somebody was dead, and he'd kicked the body. They'd blame *him*, wouldn't they? They always did. He had to get out.

With an effort he sat up, straightening his back. He was sure that everybody's eyes must be on him, that the sergeant would be looking fixedly at those shoes and the dark stain. He forced himself to look up, slowly and apparently without interest. He made himself take a deep breath.

Nobody was looking at him. The tramp at the desk was causing a lot of noise and commotion. Two other patrolmen walked through the hall to the main doors, talking about driving in the fog. Tig walked casually along with them, his hands in his pockets, his head down. Nobody noticed him go.

Once out in the street, Tig entered the fog, still thick and all-embracing, like a comforting blanket. It was wet and clammy, and it smelt strangely of old bonfires, but it was also a hiding-place. Tig ambled cautiously along for a few yards, then when the lights of the police station had become dim, he broke into a gallop. He tried to run quietly, but his shoes made a frightening uproar, even on the wet and slippy pavement. The round face of the church clock, lit from within, loomed up above him, and he darted to one of the buttresses at the side of the church porch, where the darkness was even more impenetrable than in the street. He found a wooden seat against the flint wall, and he sank down onto it, trying to breathe without making a noise. His ears were strained for any sound of pursuit, but there was none. No pattering footsteps, no echoing shout. A blessed quiet.

Gradually his breath came more easily, and his heart stopped thumping. He found, with some surprise, that he was not cold. He was content to stay there for a minute or two, and to consider what to do next. As he sat, he scraped the toe of his shoe against a tussock of grass. He felt happier when he was sure the blood was gone.

Should he go back home? His mother might wonder where he was, but there was always a chance that she might not even notice his absence. She wouldn't be back herself until late. He'd been out before and she hadn't known. Tig thought of his home life without emotion or self-pity. He knew his mother would do what she thought necessary, whenever she remembered. But he was also well aware that his presence in the house was a nuisance, and that she would not be sorry when he left for good. In any case, it was quite possible that the school had got in touch with her, and told her about the firework and his walking out of the place. It might be as well to let her simmer down a bit before he showed his face again. He'd have to choose his moment for return when the brandy had made her careless.

And then Tig thought of Harry. Harry Ward was the man who sold hot dogs from a mobile stand in the arcade by the bus station. Tig had sometimes helped Harry in the past, when trade was brisk, and Harry paid him in kind. The thought of a hot sausage, greasy, thick with onions, smoking and sizzling on the tray, all ready to be put inside a good crisp roll, made Tig's mind up for him. He felt cheered by the prospect. He was even more cheered when he rose suddenly, like a ghost, just as a courting couple, arm-in-arm, turned off the road and made for the seat. The girl squeaked and the man swore. Tig made a crude gesture and swaggered off into the fog.

Harry was on his usual pitch in the arcade. There were no customers. Harry was brooding, glaring out into the night as though it were a personal enemy. He greeted Tig curtly. Tig wondered whether to push his luck. He hung around, silent. Harry looked at him sourly.

"Lost your tongue, kid?" Harry's voice was deep, and he had what he liked to call an American accent. "You can cut those rolls, if you need a job. Not much doing now, but they'll be coming out of the flicks and the bingo later."

Thankfully, Tig got on with the job. He said nothing. Harry was deep in a long story about his landlord and a broken window, a story which was addressed to the sausages rather than to Tig, and he seemed not to want any answers to his rhetorical questions.

Later, when a coach came into the bus station, they had customers, and Tig was busy. Harry liked to keep up a patter of meaningless phrases when there were customers about. He reckoned, rightly, that it attracted trade, out of curiosity if nothing else. It was in the middle of a short rush of custom that Tig found Harry putting on an act of being cross.

"No, I shan't give you a penny for the guy," he rumbled. "Whaddya think I am? Made of money? Garn! Clear off!"

Tig looked up and saw the object of Harry's wrath. A little group of four children, pushing an open pram with a Guy Fawkes in it. Their faces were sullen and dirty. Their leader, a girl with bright bedraggled hair, stood in front of Harry, her eyes snapping with fury. Behind her were two small boys, younger and darker, and another child who might have been either a boy or girl. Harry raised a fist threateningly. The girl let fly a stream of abuse, but Harry took no more notice of her. Trade, for the moment, was more important. He was interested in taking money, not giving it away. The next time Tig looked up, the little group with the guy had gone.

When the cinema crowds had come and gone, Harry started to pack up his stand. Tig, with a hot dog in one hand, helped him. Harry had recovered his temper by now, and he gave some loose change to Tig for his trouble.

Tig mumbled his thanks and shambled off. He had no idea where he should go, or what he would do, and he was surprised when he found himself at the back gate of Pete's place. He looked at the house, but there was no light showing at any of the windows.

Tig remembered the derelict shed just inside the back fence. It might not be a palace, but it would keep him dry. He crept in through the piles of old tyres, drawing comfort from their closeness. He found some sacking, rough and evil-smelling, but warm. Within a few minutes he was asleep.

Five

IT was a ray of weak sunshine across his face that woke Tig next morning. He stirred irritably, and tried to pull the blankets closer round his lean form. Then his eyes opened wide, and he stared without comprehension at a row of old and dusty bamboo canes suspended above his head. The spiders had been busy there, and everything was covered with a fine net of grey grime.

Tig put out a hand to throw back the blankets, and the feel of the coarse sacking brought memory flooding back. He twisted over onto his knees and sat back on his ankles. The dusty light forcing its way through the cracked window-pane of the shed showed him the piles of secondhand tyres which Pete collected and hoped one day to turn into good money. There was one pane of glass missing from the window, below which a shelf held an assortment of jam jars, paint brushes and rusty nails. There was also a brown mug. Tig noticed with surprise that steam was rising gently from it.

He got to his feet and stared at the mug. He stretched out a hand: it was a real mug, and it was real coffee inside it. Tig stopped trying to work it out. He buried his nose in it. The warmth from the brown china felt good to his hands. He sat on a pile of tyres and looked out at the world.

The fog had gone. The sky was clear, and the sun was shining. There was a refreshing nip in the air. Tig was content to sit there, drink his coffee, and breathe the freshness of the air.

Pete's head appeared through the window.

"Oh, you're up," he said. "Rise and shine, sonny boy."

"How did you know I was here?" Tig asked. There were a lot of questions he wanted to ask, but this seemed the most pressing. "Thanks for the coffee," he added.

"S'all right. There's some breakfast on the way."

"Breakfast?"

"You know, food."

Tig stared at him.

"Where's it coming from?"

"What, breakfast? The kitchen, of course."

Tig made a sudden movement as if to get up and escape.

"Calm down!" Pete told him. He opened the door of the shed, and came in. He sat companionably on another pile of tyres. "Calm down, Tig. Nobody knows you're here. 'cept me."

"But how did you know?"

Pete's thin shoulders moved. "Just had a feeling," he said. "I often come down here with my breakfast. They've got used to it." He nodded his head in the direction of the house. "They call it inspecting my assets. These tyres are going to be worth something soon. I've got to get another dozen, and then I can sell the whole lot."

"Who to?"

"That'd be telling. Business secret, mate."

Pete's mother shouted from the back door.

"Breakfast's ready."

Pete eased himself through the door. In a short time he was back, his hands full of bread.

"Sausage sandwiches," he said. "Help yourself."

Tig did. They ate in silence. When the food had gone and the coffee mug was empty, Tig said, "Thanks, Pete." He played with the coffee cup, and stared at the sunshine through the grimy window. He got up.

"You off?"

"Yeah."

"Where?"

"I dunno. Back home, I suppose. I tell you," Tig sounded suddenly vicious, "I'm not going back to that school again."

"Don't blame you, mate," Pete said without emphasis. "What'll your mother say?"

"Aah, she won't notice."

"Tell you what, Tig," said Pete, as he dragged his lean frame to its feet. "What you need is a good woman to look after you, else you'll be falling down the nearest hole in the road, but until she comes along, you'll have to put up with me."

Tig stared at him. "You missing school too, then?"

"Who cares? Like your ma. Nobody'll notice. Let's go to the market."

"What are we waiting for?" said Tig.

"Me," said Pete. "I'd better take the mug back, or things'll be said. I'll see you in the lane."

Tig watched Pete saunter up the path towards the kitchen, the mug swinging from a finger. When he was out of sight, Tig slipped cautiously round the piles of old tyres and out into the lane. The rickety fences gave him plenty of cover. He still felt as though he was on the run from somebody or something, but he didn't know what. He wasn't worried about missing school — he'd done that enough times before. He'd look in at home round about the middle of the day, at the right time, so that his mother didn't suspect anything. And in the meantime, the sun was shining, and he had Harry's money in his pocket.

His shoulders went back, he stood straight, and he waited for Pete. When Pete came, he was stuffing a packet of biscuits into the pocket of his anorak.

"It'll come in useful," he said briefly.

They walked in companionable silence along the lane, and through the maze of small back-streets into the crowds of the main shopping centre. As they passed the White

Lion Hotel, Tig took a quick look down the alley, half expecting to see a black jumbled heap at the foot of the lamp standard, but everything seemed quiet and peaceful in the clear morning sunshine.

Tig suddenly ran off down the road. Pete caught him up at the doorway of a big department store.

"What got into you?" he enquired, puffing.

"There was a copper coming out of the station." Tig's face looked white.

"Well, so what? Did he recognise you?"

Tig shook his head. His eyes darted up and down the road.

"Don't think so. Never seen him before. Just don't like coppers this morning."

Pete laughed. "What have you been up to?" he asked.

"Nothing. But I went and told them about the body in the alley last night after I left you, and we went to have a look and there wasn't anything there."

"Told you so," Pete said cheerfully. "You imagined it, that's all."

Tig glared.

"What about the blood, then?"

"You fell down, knocked your head, got blood all over your face, had a bad dream. You looked scared enough when you came round to me. All white and pasty."

"Come on," said Tig. He was tired of this conversation. He was quite sure in his own mind. He *had* seen it, and the two men with the leather case, and it had *not* been his own blood on his hands. But he couldn't stand around all day trying to convince that thick-head Pete.

There were market-stalls every day of the week in the big square by the town hall. Most of them sold fruit and vegetables, but there were as well occasional oddities like clothes and second-hand books, records, brassware, pets and sweets. There was a fountain in the middle of the square, the water falling from the mouths of four fish into a shallow basin, where orange peel and old brown paper bags floated till they rotted. Broad steps led up to the fountain, smooth and worn with age. A brass plate announced the commemoration of Queen Victoria's Jubilee, but now the fountain steps were the haunt of tramps and idlers.

Tig and Pete sat on the corner of the steps, watching the crowds buying and selling in the bright sunlight.

"Well, what do we do?" Pete asked. He was beginning to regret his offer to accompany Tig's truancy. There was bound to be trouble.

Tig rolled an empty beer bottle up and down under one shoe. "Your suggestion," he said. He got up, pushed his hands in the pockets of his jeans, and sauntered off down the rows of stalls. He stopped to pick up an apple at a fruit-stall. "Give you a penny for it?" he said with a grin to the plump woman who stood behind the piled boxes. The woman was not amused. "Twenty-four a pound," she said sharply. "Take it or leave it." Tig left it.

At one corner of the square, a road led off to the back of the town hall. It had shops all along one side with a covered walk at the front of them held up by concrete pillars. The place was crowded. No traffic was allowed here, but the road was full of the noise of feet, the shouts of salesmen, and the chatter of housewives. Above the general hubbub rose the clear sounds of a flute and a violin. Tig looked round to see where the music was coming from.

A few yards down, leaning against one of the concrete pillars outside Boots, stood a man, bearded and sun-tanned. He was wearing a bright green jersey, and on his thick curly hair perched a little round woollen cap with a bobble on top. He was playing a flute. He had no music in front of him, and his eyes were closed. He seemed to have no interest in anything around him except for his music. At his feet lay an old cloth cap with a little heap of copper coins in it. Occasionally some passer-by would add a penny to the heap, but the musician seemed to take no notice.

Beside the man was a girl. She looked young, and she would have been pretty if her face had been clean. The sockets of her eyes were two black holes of make-up. Her hair was loose and floated round her shoulders. Her dress was long, shabby, and torn. She played the violin with an absorption and skill equal to the man's.

Tig watched from a short distance away. He had nothing better to do. It wasn't his kind of music, but it held within it a sense of freedom and joy which attracted him. It fitted in with his own mood. With a slight sense of embarrassment he recognised, honestly, that he *liked* their music, though he had no idea why.

Tig stood, leaning like them against a concrete pillar, feeling the rough surface against the back of his head. He wondered whether to take a coin from his pocket and chuck it in the cap, but something like self-consciousness held him back. He was content for the moment to stand and listen, his eyes on the ground.

The flute music stopped. Tig glanced up. The violinist was still playing, but the flautist had lowered his instrument. His eyes were open and he was staring with frightening intensity at Tig.

Tig stiffened. Those dark eyes, staring straight at him, even from a distance of five yards with other people streaming to and fro, made him somehow afraid. He jerked his hands out of his pockets and backed away. The man's eyes followed him. Tig found an obstruction behind him, put out a hand to push it away, and found it was Pete.

"Hey!" said Pete. "Mind where you're sticking your fists."

"Pete," said Tig, in an urgent whisper. "Turn round, and walk away. Don't run. Just look natural."

"I always do," said Pete, but he caught some of Tig's earnestness. "All right, all right mate. I'm going."

They walked slowly away. When they turned the corner into the square, Pete looked at Tig enquiringly.

"That man playing the flute," said Tig, with a strange

hesitation in his voice.

"What about him?"

"I've seen him before. I recognised him. It was one of the blokes I saw in the alley last night."

Six

PETE stared at Tig with disbelief. "Aw, come off it, Tig," he said. "That's all make-believe, remember? So you had a bad day yesterday, and you got scared in the fog, and laughed at by a copper, and you spent the night in the shed at the bottom of the garden. And it's morning, and the sun's shining, and the bad dreams are just that. Got it?"

Tig shook his head slowly. He stared straight in front of him at nothing.

"I'm going to have another look at him," he said flatly. "Just to make sure. You coming?"

Pete lifted his hands to heaven in mock prayer. "Tig, you're crazy," he said. "Dead nuts."

Tig made no answer. He walked away.

"Tig!" Pete bellowed at his retreating back. He stood irresolutely for a second, then with a muttered curse, he followed. They made their way round to the back of the shops outside which the musicians had been playing. To Pete's continued questions, all that Tig would say was, "I know what I'm doing, Pete, so shut up." Pete was indignant but helpless.

At the back of Boots there was one small door for the use of those customers who parked their cars in the multi-storey car park opposite. Tig pushed through the door.

"You sure this is the right one?" Pete asked.

Tig gave him a contemptuous glance. "Oh, you're still there, are you? Course I'm sure. There's only one Boots in this town."

Tig quickly threaded his way through the throng of shoppers till he stood just to one side of the main doors, taking cover behind a cut-out cardboard model of a large healthy female wearing a camera slung from her shoulder and little else. He seemed to be totally unaware of the incongruity of his position. Pete was very well aware of it, and just hoped that no one was looking.

"Pete," said Tig quietly.

Pete changed his weight from one foot to another, and looked a question.

"Pete," said Tig, "you stay here. I'm going out to get behind them. Back in a minute."

Pete nodded with dumb misery. He tried to look as though he was interested in the feeding instructions on a tin of dog meat. Out of the corner of his eye he watched Tig.

Tig was moving slowly and silently out through the glass door and across the sunlit pavement. His hands, as usual, were thrust in his pockets. He was trying to look casual, as though he had nothing much to do. He rested his shoulders on the concrete pillar, looking back at the shop door, and when he saw Pete's anxious face peering out over the camera girl's unclothed shoulder, he grinned and gave a thumbs-up sign. Pete was not amused.

Tig lounged round the pillar. The two musicians were only a few feet from him now. He could have put out a hand and touched them. The grin faded from his face. He could see the man's head moving in time to the music, the curly hair ruffled and falling in long waves to his shoulders. The flute seemed to engage his whole attention. The girl by his side bent down to pick up a penny that was lying loose on the pavement. She put it with the others in the cap, straightened up, and continued to play. Her long skirt swayed in time to the music. It was only a little detail, but Tig, who was watching everything, noticed that as the girl bent down she revealed a pair of surprisingly large shoes.

And there was something else. Tig's nose twitched. Something at the back of his mind struggled to get out. There was a faint scent carried on the air as the girl moved and her dress swayed. A scent that Tig knew and recognised. It carried him back to the evening before when he had stood wedged between a lamp standard and the wall, and two people had caught a case thrown from the hotel window. And in the blackness of the pavement lay a blood-streaked body.

Tig shivered. The warmth had gone out of the sun. He turned quickly with a rising sensation of fear in his throat, tripped on his own feet and went down. He scrambled up with a quick curse. As he made for the safety of the glass doors he was aware of a bright and piercing eye fixed on him from out of a mass of tangled hair.

Pete was still looking innocent behind the cardboard lady. Tig made for him. There was excitement in his eyes.

"Well?" said Pete.

"It's them," Tig whispered. "I'm sure of it now."

"What are you going to do?"

Tig said nothing. There was a frown on his face, and he stared at the cardboard model with dislike. People knocked into him, but he took no notice.

"Watch it!" Pete exclaimed. "The one with the flute is looking this way."

Tig kept his back to the glass doors.

"What's he doing?"

"Just looking."

"What are we scared of, anyway?" Tig said suddenly. "He can't touch us."

"Search me," said Pete. He sounded miserable. "It's your story, not mine."

"Keep looking," Tig told him.

The music could be heard faintly over the noise of massed voices, but there was something different about it now. Then Tig realised what it was: the violin was still playing, but the flute was not. He took a quick glance over his shoulder and saw the bearded face, and when he saw it, he grabbed Pete's arm.

"Hey! Lay off!" Pete exclaimed.

"He's coming in!" Tig whispered. "Pete, make for the back. We've got to get out. Go on, Pete, move!"

Pete jerked convulsively, and then squirmed through the crowds. Tig looked round. He had to find some way of stopping the man with the beard long enough to allow him to get out through the back without being seen. He cast a speculative eye over the ample proportions of the cardboard lady, and measured the distance between her and the piled pyramids of dog food. He pushed her gently to set her swaying. She was, he found, nicely balanced. Another quick push, and he hared off down the aisle. He hoped his judgement had been sound. He skipped round a pay desk and waited.

There was a solid thump as the cardboard lady keeled over and hit her head on the pyramid of tins. A couple of tins rolled off, bouncing a little on the way down, and then the whole structure collapsed into a sea of rolling jangling metal, filling the aisle completely. Over all the noise rose the cries of outraged shoppers.

A satisfied grin broke over Tig's face, and he exhaled a deep luxurious breath.

"That'll hold him," he said.

He dashed down the aisle towards the back door. The crowds parted before him. Some of them were massing round the fallen pyramid of dog food; others, imagining it was a bomb scare, were trying to get away as fast as possible. The conditions of chaos suited Tig fine. As he struggled through he yelled "Fire!" once or twice, knowing that it could never be traced back to him. He was enjoying himself.

Pete was waiting at the back of the shop, appalled at the commotion, but quite ignorant of its cause or cure. He just wanted to escape. He and Tig shot out of the door into the bright sunlight, and blinked.

"Which way?" Pete said.

Tig considered briefly. "To the market. We can get lost there. Just keep your head down, Pete."

He sprinted for the corner of the car park. Pete raised a despairing hand to heaven, but he began to follow, having no idea what this was all about. Something large and formidable stood in his way.

"Going somewhere, sonny?"

Pete looked up, surprised. The voice was deep, but it came from a woman. She was broad and capable and had rich orange hair. Pete put out a hand to push past. He found himself caught, swung round, and imprisoned. His arm, bent behind his back, cracked alarmingly. He let out a howl, and Tig, a few yards ahead, stopped and looked back.

"Now," said the woman with orange hair, her voice a mixture of command and complacency. "Come along back inside the shop."

"You let me go!" Pete yelled. The years slipped away from him and he felt about six. "What have I done wrong?"

"Shop-lifting," said the woman tightening her grip. Pete howled again.

"You're nuts!" Pete yelled at her. "I never took a thing."

The woman said nothing. Still holding Pete firmly with one hand, she reached round and plucked the tin of dog food from Pete's grasp. Pete gaped at it with total lack of comprehension. He couldn't think how it had got into his hands: so much had happened since he had picked it up near the cardboard lady at the front of the shop.

"Well? Are you coming quietly?" The woman jerked him forward, and Pete stumbled to the door. Tig, standing irresolute at the corner, found his mind blank. It was obvious what had happened to Pete, but it was equally obvious that he couldn't do a thing about it.

Pete was just entering the back door of the shop, his arm bent behind him, his face a picture of misery, when a girl shot out and nearly knocked him over. She was small and wiry and had long fair hair. Her fists were waving furiously.

"You pig!" she yelled at Pete.

Pete's eyes opened wide in astonishment and his jaw dropped.

"Do you know this boy?" the woman with orange hair demanded.

"Know him?" the girl screamed. "Course I do. He walked out on me!" She advanced on Pete as though to attack him. Pete just stood. The whole thing was out of his control. The girl pushed her face at his. "Count two," she whispered, "then run!" Pete found himself doing as he was told.

The girl whirled round, her head lowered, and she butted the woman firmly in the middle of her broad figure. One sharp-heeled shoe lashed out and landed on the woman's toe. Her grip on Pete momentarily slackened.

"Run!" yelled the girl.

Pete ran. So did Tig. The girl kept pace with them. In a moment they were lost in the crowds of the market square.

Seven

THEY sat in a row on the steps of the ornamental fountain in the middle of the square, Tig and Pete, and the girl between them. It was a little oasis of peace in the business of the market. There was a drunk on the other side of the fountain, waving a bottle, and singing bits of music-hall songs, but his presence, they felt, helped to take attention away from them. They were safe.

The girl was Liz Prior. She was a cousin of Tig, though he hadn't seen much of her recently. She was three years older than he was, pretty in a casual sort of way, careless of what she did or said. There had been some trouble in the past, Tig remembered, involving somebody else's money and the police. He wondered vaguely why she should suddenly pop up now to get them out of a hole.

"Can't have pals of mine done down by that orange-haired ex-police-woman," she said.

"Is that what she is?" Tig asked.

"Well, she's the store detective now."

"How do you know?"

"You get to find out these things."

"Well, thanks anyway," Tig said.

"That's OK. Shouldn't you two be at school?"

Tig scrabbled his feet among the litter round the fountain.

"Ah, I see, playing hookey. And a nice morning for it.

Well cheerio. Got to see a man at the *Evening Herald.* He's a reporter. He and me — well, you know, we go around together. Least, *he* thinks so."

She started off through the market. Tig and Pete tagged along behind.

"Did you say the *Evening Herald*?" Tig asked as they came into the High Street.

"That's it. Office over there."

"Is today's paper out yet?"

"It hits the streets about twelve. Too early yet. Did you want one?"

"Just an idea," said Tig.

"Well, they're in the office about eleven. I can get you one if you like. It'll cost you eight whole pennies."

Tig dug into the pockets of his jeans.

"Thanks, man," said Liz. "You hang about here, and I'll be back."

Tig watched her weave her way through the traffic to the doors of the *Evening Herald* office.

In a minute or two she appeared from behind a bus, carrying a copy of the paper.

"All yours," she announced.

"Thanks."

"Forget it," said Liz cheerfully. "Can't stop now. But you can buy me a coffee if you like at half-past one. At Rose's. Be good." She darted away through the traffic.

Pete sniffed.

"Some hope," he said scornfully. "Nothing like asking, is there? What are you looking for, Tig?"

Tig was flipping through the pages. People squeezed past on the narrow pavement, and knocked into him with shopping baskets, but he stayed where he was, one foot on the kerb, one in the gutter. Pete hovered. Tig moved on a yard or two, and found a bus stop to lean against.

"Pete," he said, "listen to this."

"Didn't know you could read," Pete remarked.

"Belt up, Pete, and listen. It's in the stop press column

on the back page. 'Robbery at White Lion Hotel', that's the heading. 'A collection of valuable silver and gold coins, part of an exhibition mounted at the White Lion Hotel by the something-or-other society, was reported stolen this morning. The police are making enquiries. The coins are valued at several thousand pounds.' That's all."

Pete craned his long neck over Tig's shoulder to read the small smudged paragraph for himself.

"Cor!" was his only comment.

"So, you see," said Tig, "I *was* right. I bet you anything you like that's what I saw last night. Those two and the case being chucked out of the window. I knew there was something funny going on. I *saw* them. The bloke with the beard, and the girl who was playing the violin. I recognised the scent she had on. I *saw* them."

"Hang on a second, Tig," said Pete. "You saw them, that's OK. But they saw you as well, remember?"

Tig did remember. He folded the paper carefully, and put it away in a pocket of his jacket. His brain was a mass of confused pictures, like an unfinished jig-saw puzzle, but there was one piece which stared at him clearly — the man with the beard and the piercing eyes. It wasn't a bad dream, and it wasn't a game. It was for real.

Tig looked up and down the street.

"Can you see them?" he asked Pete.

"Who?"

"Don't be thick, Pete. Those musicians. They're the ones who pulled that job. They know me. And they must realise that I recognised them after what happened in the shop. They'll be after me."

Pete looked serious.

"What are you going to do?"

Tig stared at the traffic with unseeing eyes. Then he pulled the paper out of his pocket, unfolded it, and, despite the crowds round him and Pete's insistent demand to know what he thought he was doing, Tig read carefully the headlines on every page. At length, with a puzzled sigh, he put the paper away again.

"Well?" said Pete.

"There's nothing there." Tig sounded disappointed.

"What about?"

"The body," said Tig simply. "You'd have thought there'd be something about that."

"But you said there *wasn't* a body," Pete protested. "Not when you looked afterwards."

"There wasn't. But it can't just disappear. It must be somewhere."

"Are you sure the guy was dead?"

"Pretty sure," Tig said shortly.

"You'll have to tell them about the coins."

"Tell who?"

"The police."

"Oh yeah? And are they going to believe me? After last night? No chance. I *did* tell them I saw a couple of people, but they didn't seem to take much notice." Tig glared at the passing shoppers as though he'd like to kick them. Pete looked at him helplessly.

Tig shook himself free from doubts.

"Tell you what," he said. "We'll go across the common. You still got that packet of biscuits?"

"Sure."

"Good. I'm hungry. We'll see if my ma's at home."

Pete looked doubtful. "Do you think that's a good idea?"

"Sure," said Tig. "I want support. If she starts throwing things, remember to duck."

But Tig's mother was not at home. Tig did not have his own key to the little terrace-house, but he knew where the spare key was always kept — under a flower-pot in the corner of the back yard. He let himself in. There was a note for him on the kitchen table, telling him where to find a couple of pork-pies. He found them. He and Pete sat on the back doorstep and ate.

"I told you so," said Tig without emotion. "She never even knew I wasn't there last night."

Pete looked at him sideways, but made no reply.

"It's never been the same," Tig went on, "since Dad walked out. Got those biscuits?"

They munched in silence.

Tig twisted round to see the kitchen clock through the window. Then he searched through his pockets and laid out all the money he had in a line along the doorstep. Pete looked at him enquiringly.

"It'll do," Tig said. He swept up the money, put it back in his pocket, and stood up.

"Where you off to?"

"Coffee," said Tig. "With Liz. At Rose's. We'll just make it. Have to run."

Rose's was a small café just off the High Street, catering for the cheap trade. Liz was already there. Tig breathed a silent sigh of relief. He had been prepared to buy the girl coffee if necessary, but if she'd already paid for it herself, well, so much the better.

He bought two cups of coffee at the counter, and they joined Liz at a table in the window.

"Howdy, stranger," said Liz. "I'll treat you next time."

Tig grinned feebly. Pete drank his coffee with a determination which prevented all other action. He had decided to leave the talking to Tig.

Tig as well was busy with his own thoughts. He was trying to make up his mind whether to tell Liz all about it. Pete was a nice guy, but not even his best friends would call him bright. He was in the same year as Tig at the school they attended when they felt like it, but there was a special class for people like Pete. Good with his hands, though, and a keen fisherman. But definitely not the boy-wonder of the modern age. Perhaps, Tig thought, it might be better to have another head working for him.

"Go on," said Liz suddenly. "Ask me. What's going to win the 2.30?"

Tig twisted the cup between his fingers.

"It's a long story," he started.

Liz looked at her watch.

"Cut it," she advised. "I've got till two. I'll give you four minutes."

Tig made up his mind to trust her. He told her the whole story in short abrupt sentences. When he finished, he looked up at Liz's face to see whether she was laughing. He was relieved to find she wasn't. She looked serious and grave and somehow comforting.

"So you think," said Liz, after a moment, "that you can't tell the police, because they wouldn't believe you, not after last night. So you've got to get evidence. Right?"

Tig nodded.

"And your only clue is the two musicians who were after you when I came along and did my rescue act. Well, it's a start. But about the other thing, the body that disappeared. Is that anything to do with this coin robbery, d'you reckon?"

"Might be," said Tig. "But the body was there before the two blokes came along, that I'm sure of."

"But they might have been there before you arrived, gone off, and then come back."

"I hadn't thought of that," said Tig.

"Well, start thinking," said Liz. "It's your problem, you solve it. I've gotta go, and when you've gotta go, you've gotta go. Tell you what, I'll be here at eleven sharp tomorrow morning. With tomorrow's first edition. Then if anything has turned up, you'll know. All clear?"

Liz got up and made for the door. They saw her cross the road and run out of sight.

"D'you think she's all right?" Pete asked diffidently.

"All right?"

'Well, you know, d'you think you can trust her?"

Tig laughed. "Course she's all right. I tell you, Pete, she's right about one thing."

"What's that?"

"When she said the only clue was the two musicians. Well, they may have gone to ground, but if they haven't, they should be easy to find. You don't have to look, you just listen."

"You going to look, then?"

Tig stared. "Sure," he said.

Pete looked worried. "You going home tonight?" he asked.

"I'll consider it."

"What are you going to do now?"

"Go and look for 'em. You coming?"

"Don't mind."

"Good."

They went.

Eight

THE sun was still shining as they left Rose's café, but it was a weak and miserable effort. The air felt damp, and mist could be seen rising from the streets.

"It'll be foggy again," Pete said.

"Cheerful," Tig remarked.

They walked up and down the High Street, looking into shop windows and discussing what they would buy if they had the money. Tig jingled a few odd coppers in his pocket to keep himself cheerful, but it was not much good.

The light faded rapidly. The street lamps came on and fought a useless battle with the twilight. Banks of fog began to roll down the streets. It was wet and it smelt foul. Tig felt like giving up. Indeed, he had to stop and think once or twice just what it was they were supposed to be looking for, and in any case, he asked himself, what was the point? He'd have to go back to school some time, he supposed. Better to get it over with. Pete seemed to be thinking along the same lines.

"D'you think they've noticed?" he said. "Up at the school?"

"Might have. It'll be 'on report' again for you and me. That and two sides of best hand-writing promising not to do it again. Oh, well!" Tig shrugged his shoulders with an expressive gesture. "Who cares?"

"You going on much longer?" Pete asked.

"A bit."

They trailed down side-streets, and back again, and up to the station, round the square, and back down the High Street, but they caught no sight of the two musicians, nor did they hear a note of their music. It was becoming more and more difficult to make out the faces of people only a few yards away. People blurred into outlines and shapes with no individual detail, the predominant colour being a soulless grey.

Tig was depressed.

"OK," he said finally. "I give in. We've been at it for a couple of hours. I'm going home."

Pete shuffled his feet and looked embarrassed.

"Tig," he said, "can you do something for me?"

"What?"

"You know, a few months back, you took a couple of days off, and you wrote a sick note, and it got past. Remember?"

"Sure," said Tig, with a grin. "All it needs is a decent bit of paper, a good pen, and some practice. Do you want one for yourself?"

"Yes," said Pete simply.

"You're on," said Tig.

"See you at school tomorrow?"

"Yep."

"What about Liz and the coffee?"

Tig swore. "I forgot. Well, she can get someone else to buy it for her. See you tomorrow."

"You'll have the note ready?" Pete was anxious.

"Five to nine. Outside the gate. Don't worry."

They parted.

Tig's mother was in the kitchen when he got home. She was at the sink doing some washing. She looked up briefly when he came in, but said nothing more than, "Wipe your boots properly." Tig did so, wondering just how much she knew, and where he should start. He decided to leave it to her to begin any conversation. He went to the bread-bin on the dresser, got out a couple of slices, and started making himself a marmite sandwich.

Mrs English dried her arms on a rough brown towel. She turned round and faced him over the kitchen table.

"Couldn't wait I see. And I had some eggs and bacon for your tea."

Tig's eyes opened wide with surprise, but he made no reply. Mrs English bustled about at the gas cooker.

"Well, sit down then. You can wait ten minutes, can't you?"

"You needn't bother," Tig mumbled. He usually got his own tea.

"Don't you tell me what to do," his mother snapped. "Sit down and shut up."

Tig did so. Ten minutes later a large plate covered with fried eggs, bacon, and bread was plumped down in front of him. He picked up his knife and fork. An appetising smell filled his nostrils.

"Now you eat that," his mother said curtly. "I know you haven't had a proper meal all day."

Tig glanced up warily. He wondered just what this last remark was supposed to mean. How much did she know?

"Thanks, Mum," he said. It seemed safest. He filled his mouth with eggs and bacon and discovered that he was very hungry. Mrs English watched him eat in grim silence.

"Well?" she said, when Tig pushed the empty plate away. "Out with it."

Tig tried to look innocent.

"Out with what, Mum?"

"Don't come that with me. You've not been at school the last two days."

So she knew, Tig said to himself. Well, it was a sort of relief, in a way. It saved having to be careful about the details of the story he made up. There was one thing, though, that he might as well put right.

"I was there yesterday morning," he said defensively.

"Yes, and then you walked out."

So she knew that too.

"Well, he was getting at me. It wasn't my fault," Tig muttered.

His mother snorted. "That's what you always say."

"Well, it's true," Tig persisted. "He was just picking on me because I'm the smallest. He always does." Then he added, "How do you know?"

"They've been around. This afternoon. From up the school."

Tig sat in silence thinking. He *could* trot out all the usual excuses for not going to school, like being bored, and wanting a bit of freedom, but there didn't seem much point. There wouldn't be any use in forging a sick note now, either — still, he could do one for Pete. It might pass. Meanwhile, he just wished the whole thing was over and finished with. It didn't occur to him to tell his mother about the two thieves and the body in the alley. Tig had never found it easy to talk to his mother — not since his father had gone, anyway. They didn't seem to have anything in common, apart from the same roof. He wondered how he could get out without a lot of fuss.

"That Mr Oakham came, with another man."

Tig groaned.

"Wanted to know where you were, they did."

"What did you tell 'em?"

"What could I? *I* didn't know. You never told me."

"You weren't here yesterday evening," Tig began.

"That's it. It's *my* fault, I suppose. You know I had the ladies' darts match, and I couldn't let them down. It's not my fault."

Tig got up and went to the sink with his plate. He knew this conversation by heart, and he knew that the ladies' darts team was just his mother's usual excuse for a night's solid drinking. Not that she ever needed much of an excuse. But then, Tig thought, she was just keeping up appearances. Like himself, and his excuses.

He ran the plate under the tap. Above the noise of the water, he heard his mother sob. That's it, Tig said to himself, and this is the point when she turns the taps on. He turned round.

"I'll make you a cup of tea," he offered. He found the kettle, filled it, and put it on the stove. It always ended like this. He supposed it was just one of those things people grew out of. He hoped so anyway.

He made the tea and poured out a cup for his mother, pushing the packet of sugar towards her hands.

Suddenly Tig realised that his mother was really crying, not in the usual make-believe fashion she used for effect, but with an open abandon that shocked him. He put one hand on her shoulder, but she shrugged him off. He didn't know what to say or do. He stood behind her, wishing he was somewhere else. He was aware that his mother was talking, but he tried hard not to listen. He could see her shoulders shaking and her fingers rubbing her eyelids, and he could see her tears falling in little wet patches on the stained tea-cloth.

He put his hand on her shoulder again.

"It's all right, Mum," he said softly, like someone talking to a sleeping baby. "It's all right. Don't cry. I'm sorry."

She covered his hand with one of hers.

"You'll go to school tomorrow?" she pleaded, her eyes ugly with tears.

"All right, Mum, don't you worry. I'll go."

"Promise?"

"It's a promise, Mum. It's all right."

Her grasp on his hand loosened, and she produced from her sleeve a tattered handkerchief. Without another word she left the kitchen. Tig could hear her steps going up the uncarpeted stairs and across the floor above him.

He stood by the table, his face set in an angry scowl. It was just not fair, he thought. He'd been through all this before. He knew she got like this at a certain stage, when she'd had a good bit to drink, but not quite enough. And what could he do? It wasn't as though he had all the money in the world to refill the empty brandy bottles in the cupboard. And he wouldn't do it if he had. A few more drinks and she would pull herself together. A few more after that she'd be flat out, it didn't matter where.

Anger, blind and unreasoning, born of complete helplessness, filled his head. He went to the cupboard where he knew she kept her supplies. Empties. A shelf-ful of empties. He found a glass, opened all the bottles and drained them into it. The result was an inch of spirit. He held it to his nose, half-inclined to drink it himself. But the smell reminded him of the effect it had on his mother. He wiped the rim of the glass carefully, and took it upstairs. His mother was lying on the bed, her eyes closed. Tig looked at her for a moment. His anger and his sense of helplessness did not lessen. He put the glass down on the little table by the bed and walked away, closing the door softly behind him.

He went downstairs, finished the washing-up, hung up the towel, gave a last look round. He had no idea why he should do so. Then he opened the back door and went out.

His old bike, rusty and tarnished, lay against the fence at the back. He patted the saddle as though it was an old friend for whom he felt a long-held affection. More than anything else in the world he wanted freedom, the freedom to go where he liked without being bothered by emotions he could neither understand nor control. He wanted *out*.

He made for the common. The common was a square of land, unaccountably left behind by the unsteady growth of the town. It was surrounded by houses and small factories, and crossed by a number of wandering paths which met and parted at unexpected places. Once it had been a golf-course, and the curious could still point out the tees and fairways and bunkers, long overgrown by coarse grass and shrub. Now it was a rubbish-dump, not one of those dumps efficiently managed by a conscientious council but haphazard, unofficial, and all-embracing. It was made of plastic crisp bags and the skeletons of ancient vehicles.

In the middle was a pyramid which Tig had watched grow larger and larger over the last few days. The local children from the houses round had built it with patience in order to see it be transformed into a towering column of black smoke and orange flame on Guy Fawkes night.

It was here that Tig found the freedom he craved. He rode his bike furiously at all obstacles with a fierce determination to overcome them or be overcome. When he forced the machine to the top of a sudden bump in the ground, he was filled with an overwhelming elation. He shouted and he yelled as loud as his lungs would let him. Once or twice he landed on the ground, once in a puddle of dirty and stinking water, but he didn't care. He picked himself up, shook himself, shook the bike, and was off again. He could feel the wind in his spiky hair. It rushed at him, like a large playful dog, and grabbed the shouts from his mouth, and threw them away into the surrounding fog.

Night had come, unlit by moon or stars. There was a strange dull opalescence from the lights of houses and streets round about, but the ground beneath him was merely different shades of darkness. A fierce joy filled Tig's brain, replacing the anger he had felt before. He was wet through, soaked to the skin with fog and muddy water, but it meant nothing to him.

He was circling round and round the pyramid of wood and combustible rubbish when he became aware of a darker shadow at the foot of it, angular and inexplicable. He stopped the bike with a violent push of his feet into the soft grass, and jumped off. It was an old pram, and there seemed to be something in it. He put out a hand to touch it, but a beam of light shot out from the blackness and hit his eyes sideways. He wheeled round, sudden panic knocking at his chest. He was aware of a little circle of children moving slowly and steadily in towards him. There were three or four of them, their white faces staring out from behind the glare of the torch held in the hand of one of them, a girl of about ten or eleven, with red hair.

"Give us a penny for the Badden," the girl with the torch whined. "Just a penny for the guy."

Tig expelled a breath of relief. He reached for his bike, got on the saddle, and said, "What guy?"

The torch swung round to light up the dilapidated pram. It was good life-like guy, solid and secure. The head was bound with a red and white scarf, and there was a grotesque plastic face that stared out with lifeless eyes.

"Give us a penny for the guy," the girl with the torch whined. "Just a penny for the guy."

Tig felt in his trouser pocket. "Here you are," he said. The coin fell to the ground noiselessly, and the beam of the torch followed its flight. Small hands scrabbled in the grass to retrieve it. Tig rode off.

He was feeling better now. The heavy weight of anger had gone from him. When he was tired, he would go home and fall into bed and forget. But he wasn't tired yet. He had very little idea what time it was, but that didn't matter. The regular stamp of his feet on the pedals gave him a strange feeling of security. He found one of the narrow tarmacked paths, and he raced down it just to see how fast he could go. There was a stile at the end of it, and he screwed the bike round in an effort to stop in time. His front wheel banged against the wooden step. The barbed wire at the side of the stile scraped his thigh, and he fell.

He found his mouth full of water, and he laughed as he spat it out. Just another muddy puddle, and he had to find it with his face. He sat up, and was aware of the water soaking through his jeans. He laughed again, but over his laughter he heard something which made his senses freeze, taking his memory back to the darkness of the alley where he had stood between the lamp standard and the wall.

Footsteps were slowly approaching along the path. Two pairs of feet, their sound oddly clarified by the foggy air because there was nothing else to hear. One pair soft and solid and slow; the second faster, clicking and tapping, to keep pace with the longer strides of the other.

Nine

FORLORN as a forsaken puppy, Pete waited at the entrance to the school for a quarter of an hour until the bell went. He had arrived earlier than usual because he did not want to miss Tig, or, more important, the sick note which Tig had promised to write for him. He had complete faith in Tig's abilities in this direction, but he did want to be sure that when he faced the class teacher at nine o'clock he had the required form of words written and spelt correctly. He paced up and down in the cold misty air, waiting.

When five to nine came, and Tig did not appear, he was not particularly worried. Hundreds of children swarmed round the main gates, having walked up the hill or being decanted from fleets of buses. It was possible, Pete thought, that Tig might be a minute or two late. No more than that, for lateness would attract attention and draw suspicion to the forged sick notes. It was even possible that Pete had missed him in the crowds: he was only a little bloke, after all. But it was unlike Tig to forget a promise: he didn't like letting his mates down, Pete was certain of that.

But when the bell went, Pete could wait no longer. He took one last look down the hill, hoping against hope that he would spot Tig's thin figure charging up, and then sprinted for his own classroom. He arrived just in time to fumble his way through the lines of battered desks to his own place. After the roll had been called, he would, he knew, be asked the reason for his absence yesterday, and sure enough the request came. Pete took a deep breath, and said he'd been sick. And where was the note to prove it? Pete made a pretence of looking through his pockets, and muttered that he must have left it at home. He was not much of a liar, and he received a long look of disbelief from the class teacher. He was told to bring the note tomorrow without fail. Pete said, "Yes, sir," and relapsed into his corner with a feeling that he was out of trouble for the moment at any rate.

It was funny about Tig, though. Of course, he might have been held up, a bit of fuss with that mother of his perhaps. He might have had to go straight to his own classroom. Pete had an idea. He put up his hand and asked permission to go to see Mr Oakham. He got another sharp look and was asked the reason. Pete thought desperately, then he said:

"I've got to hand in some extra work, sir."

This seemed a very probable reason and it passed muster. Pete left the classroom. So far, so good. Now he had to think up some excuse to hand out to old Okkerd. He knocked at the door, went in, and asked politely for the loan of a piece of chalk for his own classroom. He was reasonably certain that old Okkerd didn't notice who he was. As usual, Mr Oakham had trouble on his hands with his own class and looked far too worried to think of anything else. While he was waiting for the chalk, he took a quick look round. Thirty pairs of eyes met his with indifference, but there was no Tig. Pete made his escape.

The morning dragged on. Pete's mind was even less on his work than usual. Hard words rolled off his back like water.

It was in the break that the news got round, with the speed normal in a school, that the police were on the premises. They wanted to know where Tig was. Mr Oakham himself got hold of Pete, as a known friend of Tig's, and tried to get the truth out of him. Pete was defensive, and said as little as he could. Tig had told him that he'd given a false name to the police, so how could they be after him now? What was that name he said he'd used? French — that was it. Well, it obviously hadn't taken the police long to see through that one. French equalled English.

Pete racked his brains the rest of the morning, wondering what to do.

In the dinner hour he thought of Rose's. Liz seemed to go to Rose's Café, and she might know where Tig was. She had said she would be there at eleven, at any rate. Tig might have kept that date, as he had not been at school. It was worth a chance. Pete lumbered round the corner and into the back-street where Rose dispensed entertainment to the thirsty traveller.

The place was crowded. The smell of fried sausages, eggs, chips and anything else that could be cooked in that particular way, hung over the heads of the diners. The air was thick with smoke, and the noise was inordinate. Pete peered through the congested atmosphere, but he could not see her. He was half afraid that he might not recognise her anyway.

He pushed through to the counter.

"Is Liz about?" he asked, finding unexpected confidence.

The woman behind the counter looked at him incuriously and pointed with a dirty thumb to a corner behind the door.

"Oh thanks" Pete mumbled, turning away.

"Tea or coffee?" the woman snapped. She knew that the café was often a meeting-place for those romantically or even criminally inclined, but an entrance fee was expected, and that was the price of a cup of something hot, tasteless, and innocuous. You didn't have to eat when you came to Rose's, but you were expected to drink.

"Coffee," Pete said, searching his pockets for the necessary change.

He took his cup, its contents splashing liberally into the saucer, to the corner where Liz was contemplating a plate containing one sausage roll. She looked up and smiled.

"Better late than never, Lofty," she remarked, making room for him on the long plastic-covered seat. "The arrangement was eleven o'clock, if you recall."

Pete blushed. "Sorry," he muttered, and buried his face in the cup of coffee.

"Well, what happened then? And where's little Titch?"

"He's called Tig," Pete corrected.

"Joke, Lofty, it was a joke. Come on, let's see you smile! That's better. Where is he?"

"Dunno," Pete said. "I wondered if he'd been here. I thought you might know."

"I can't keep tabs on everybody," Liz said lightly. "He hasn't kept the date, that's all I know."

Pete looked at the steamy window. He wondered whether he ought to tell Liz, whether Tig would mind if he did. But then Tig had told her pretty well everything yesterday, so he could hardly object. And anyway, where *was* Tig?

Pete was worried, though he tried not to think so, and, as he always did when he was worried, he made up his mind to share his troubles. It all came tumbling out of him, the note that Tig had promised to write for him, Tig's absence from school, even after his promise to be there, and the police at the school. It was disjointed and nervous, but Liz listened with her head on one side and her eyes fixed on Pete's face.

When he finished, she played with a spoon for a moment before she said. "What's he got himself into, Lofty? Do you know?"

Pete shrugged. "Dunno. Nothing more than I've told you. Unless he was keeping something back. But where *is* he?"

Liz's eyes were grave.

"I think he's in something deep," she said at length. "All

this stuff about cops and robbers — it's not real."

"But that *was* real," Pete urged. "It was in the paper. The White Lion Hotel. Something about gold and silver coins from an exhibition."

"Sure it was real. And so's this." Liz pulled a crumpled newspaper from a pocket and spread it out over the stained table. "Today's *Evening Herald*. It's not a big story. Yet — There, read it." She directed Pete to a couple of paragraphs at the bottom of the front page. Pete read them and looked up puzzled.

"I don't see what it's got to do with Tig."

"Then listen, Lofty. One of the *Herald*'s news-sellers disappears, right? So who cares? Nobody. He was all by himself, had nobody to look after and nobody to look after him. Just a little midget who sold papers from a wooden shed down the street by the side of the White Lion."

Pete looked up quickly, but Liz went on.

"He hasn't been seen for two days, not since the evening of the day before last. And that was when Tig said he saw a body in the alley. Got it, brother?"

Ten

TIG'S eyes opened suddenly. He stared with total lack of comprehension at a grey and dusty beam of wood suspended above his head like the luggage-rack in a train. The engine pulsated and lurched with a regular rhythm which was at once satisfying and painful. The loud peaks of the noise were hammer-blows on an anvil, and the anvil was inside his head. It ached and throbbed, and the light hurt his eyes. He went on staring at the wooden beam, trying to remember where he was.

He had heard footsteps coming along the path on the common. That was it. And he'd crashed into the stile with his bike. He'd better find that bike, it was the only one he had. But the beam above him didn't look like the stile, and in any case he shouldn't be able to see it. It ought to be dark. And foggy. Why wasn't it dark?

Tig pulled himself to his feet, and found that although he had gone through all the necessary and laborious motions in his mind, he was still lying flat on his back, and the beam was still above him. A whole network of beams, with spiders' webs in the corners. Why couldn't he get up? He *wanted* to. Something was holding him down. Or somebody?

His eyes travelled along one of the black beams and came to rest on a window, small and grimy, through which a little miserly light pushed its way. He'd be late for school if he didn't get up. And he'd promised he would be there today. But what had happened to the footsteps?

And then there came to him, with an intensity that was shocking in its suddenness, the realisation that he ached all over. But that was silly. He never caught the flu. Why should he ache?

With an effort he shook the mists away. He was in a room, a curious circular room with stone walls and a beamed roof low over his head. One little square window threw light onto his face. There was a heap of sacking and he was lying on it. Long hard bars, like the ribs of a bed, except that there was no bed, passed under his body and over his chest. He squinted down and saw rope.

He was tied up. But that sort of thing couldn't happen to him. What had he done to deserve being tied up with rope? The memory of the musician with the staring eyes came back to him. There had been no smile in those eyes, and no smile hidden behind that straggling beard.

Tig wriggled. The movement brought life back to his body and determination to his mind. He bent his head forward to reach the rope across his chest with his teeth. His fingers explored the knots that bound his arms to his side. He felt a sudden gust of irritation which jerked him into a sitting position. That was better. He could get at the rope behind his back now. It seemed important to get those ropes off — now, before anyone came. Would anyone come? Tig was motionless while the thought of solitude burrowed into his brain, then he set to with a sort of desperate energy to free himself.

It was easier work than he had expected. The rope's tightness abruptly melted away, and he found his arms free. There was more rope round his ankles, but that was easy now, though his fingers were stiff and cold. He rubbed his legs, until the sensation of pins and needles told him that he was still alive. He had begun to wonder about that.

He was scared that he might have broken something, and was putting off the moment when he put the weight on his feet in case it might be true. But the aching in his bones was beginning to go. His head still ached, but he could see clearly now. The glittering stars and black and white chessboard patterns behind his eyes had disappeared.

Tig swung himself round till he was kneeling. His hands supported him: he could feel the rough grain of the wood between his fingers. Slowly he hoisted himself to his feet.

He looked at the heap of sacking and the lengths of coarse thick rope, and he laughed, a short soundless laugh. His mouth was as dry as sawdust.

But the rope. Somebody must have tied him up and brought him here. And where was he? He could remember nothing after the footsteps on the common path, and the remembrance of these, insistent and frightening, made him look round with quick apprehension. But there was nobody there. He bent to pick up the rope, wondering again at the ease with which he had got out of it. Funny, that. He would have been rolling about for hours if he'd been tied up properly. He remembered once, when he was very young, that a gang of kids had chained someone to a tree at the back of the playing-field. They'd all danced round him like so many painted Indians. He'd struggled until he cried, but he couldn't get away from that tree. They'd pretended to go away and leave him, and then he'd gone completely still, and they'd been scared and let him go. But it hadn't been like that, this time. It was almost as though he was *supposed* to set himself free. But if that was so, what was the point of tying him up in the first place?

Tig shook himself like a dog, realising too late that any movement produced pain. He rubbed his back against the stone wall and found the sensation pleasant.

There was something strange over the other side of the room. He hadn't noticed it before because it lay out of the sun. Tig experimentally put one foot in front of the other, found that it was an easy thing to do, and stumbled over to the white square of cotton material which had caught his eye. It was a handkerchief, clean and uncreased. There was a bulge underneath it which looked like a number of circles. Tig kicked the handkerchief away — he had tried bending down to pick it up, but his head had suddenly opened and shut like a trap-door — and found underneath it a soup-plate containing three bread rolls and a cup of what appeared to be milk.

Tig looked at these things with curiosity tinged with fear. He had obviously been meant to get himself out of those ropes and to find the food, or it would never have been placed there. He had a momentary feeling that someone was playing with him, that someone was standing just outside his sight and laughing at him. But there was nowhere for anyone to hide. The room was bare, without even a door.

And then these bread rolls and the milk. Tig lowered himself gently to the floor and looked at them. He could think of two possible solutions to the problem: first that he was supposed to eat them because they were poisoned and someone wanted him dead; secondly, that he was supposed to eat them, because they were all right, and someone wanted him to be kept alive. Why?

He'd seen two people in the dark alley, and he'd recognised those two people as the musicians playing in the street by the market the next day. He was fairly certain they'd recognised him. They'd come after him into the shop. They must have been following him all day. Those footsteps on the common path belonged to the musicians. They must have got him as he lay in the mud by the stile. And then brought him here, to be out of the way.

Another picture sprang into Tig's mind, the picture of the blood-stained face on the pavement, lit for one brief second by the yellow light of a torch. Somebody had been killed in that alley. Somebody had wanted that battered face out of the way too.

Mechanically, Tig stretched out a hand for one of the bread rolls. If those musicians had wanted him dead, there were easier ways than putting arsenic in his breakfast.

Anyway, he was hungry.

As he ate, and as movement returned more easily to his body, Tig let his imagination wander over the possibilities. He was in a room, with food, and with liberty, but with a number of real or supposed dangers to work his way through, like one lone soldier through a minefield. He didn't underestimate his opponents: he had been scared by them, and he was sensible enough to know it. Tig had always spent a lot of his time putting up resistance to opponents. It made a change to have a different set of enemies and a different kind of battle. He liked a good fight: it was nice to know that he had some chance of winning this one. When he was fighting his usual opponents in school, the dice always seemed to be loaded in favour of the teachers.

It all came back to one disconcerting question. Why wasn't he dead? He wasn't indestructible. A good knock on the head would have done it. Well, he had a lump on his forehead, but that was nothing to worry about. Not like the one that poor bloke in the alley had copped. And he could have done it himself, when he slipped in the mud by the stile.

And if they had killed him, what would they have done with the body? A corpse lying about in the path soon gets noticed by someone. *He* had seen that corpse in the alley.

But then, that corpse had disappeared. Tig let his brain work over that problem for a bit. Without thinking, he put out a hand for another roll, and found he'd eaten them all. Well, there was still the milk. He drank it, and found to his surprise it was almost fresh.

What day was it? By the look of the sun, it was early morning, but he might have been lying there, or somewhere else, for more than just one night. The freshness of the milk didn't prove it either way. He thought of his watch. It *was* early morning: his watch was still working. He knew it only went for a day and a half without winding: he usually wound it up when he went to bed, and he certainly had not wound it the night he crashed into the stile.

That was better. He was getting on. He sat with his back against the stone wall, his eyes narrowed against the light from the little window.

So what *did* you do with a body? Tig tried to put himself in the place of the person who had done it. No, he couldn't think that way. He was all kinds of fool, a good many people had told him so, but he was not that kind.

Bury it?

Where?

Throw it in the canal.

Wouldn't it float?

Hide it in a trunk.

And where do you hide the trunk?

Put it some place where nobody ever went.

Like this round room he was in.

But he was alive, wasn't he?

Burn it.

Some fire!

How much wood or coal would you need?

Tig sat as still as stone.

Into his mind came one vivid picture. A great high pyramid of wood, soaked in petrol. Somebody throwing a match. Leaping flames dancing up, consuming and destroying whatever they touched. Orange light and yellow sparks, up, up into the night sky till the stars themselves grew dark. And on top of the pyramid the figure of a man, shabby, grotesque, his clothes alight, the flames licking at his hair. All around people standing and watching, enjoying the heat from the blazing timber, laughing at each other, as the figure at the top gradually slithered down into the red seething heart of the fire . . .

And nobody knowing it wasn't just a pair of trousers and a jacket stuffed with straw.

Last night, at the foot of the bonfire, he had seen a pram with a Guy Fawkes figure in it. A well-made and solid figure. Its head had been wrapped in a red and white scarf and its face was a monstrous pink mask.

And today was November the fifth. People *expected* a body to be burned on November the fifth, all part of a make-believe bit of history. They would have their body.

Tig sat on, watching the light from the window crawl across the floor, wondering if it could really happen that way, thinking of the little group of children who had been there with the pram and the guy. A penny for the guy.

There had been a girl there too, small, with gleaming red hair. But she'd been just a kid . . .

Abruptly Tig sprang to his feet. When he'd told the police about the body in the alley, they hadn't believed him. He didn't reckon any of the others he'd told had really believed him either. He was beginning to think he didn't believe it himself. But there was one way to find out, to make sure, to settle the thing in his own mind. It didn't matter about anybody else.

And in order to do that, he must somehow get out of this round stone room.

Eleven

TIG looked round his circular prison. The one thing that would have been most useful, a door, was missing, but there was a window. It was small and dirty, and if it had ever opened it resisted Tig's determined pressure now. He thought about breaking the glass, but what he could see through the grimy panes was not reassuring: the tops of trees and a featureless sky. He must be some way up.

He stepped back, with the idea of throwing something at the glass to break it, except that there seemed nothing obvious to use. His heel hit something which before had escaped his notice, the edge of a trap-door. Tig scrabbled with his fingers at the planks, but all he succeeded in doing was breaking a nail. He cursed as he sat back on his heels, considering his next move. It wasn't going to be as easy as all that.

He had a pen-knife in his pocket. He extended the biggest blade and inserted it into the crack, but it became clear that the metal would break before the wood. Then he began to scrape away at it, carving slices and little chunks, fearful that after all the blade might snap. It was a relief to find the wood soft and rotten.

After a few minutes of careful work Tig had cleared enough wood to put the fingers of one hand through. He knelt to one side of the trap-door and tugged, but however much force he exerted it seemed to make no difference: the trap-door remained obstinately firm. It must have been bolted from below.

Tig was annoyed. He got up and stamped as hard as he could. The wood shook but it stood firm. A cloud of fine dust rose from the timbers to clog his nostrils.

He lay down to put an eye to the hole he had made. All he could see was another floor below, covered with the same fine grey dust, and what looked like the edge of another trap-door.

Just what sort of building *was* this? It was round and made of stone, and it had several wooden floors, but no doors. Tig forced his brain to work. It was something in the shape of the walls that gave him the clue. As his eye travelled up the rough surface, the walls seemed to be bending in towards him, narrower at the ceiling than at the floor.

A light-house?

But they couldn't have taken him that far. It was miles to the coast. Or had they?

Then he remembered years ago being taken on a trip by an old teacher as part of a history course. They'd been to the ramparts of a castle, to a museum in the afternoon, and ended up by exploring the ruins of another building. Large, tall, circular, with great wooden sails like a cross standing against light blue sky. They'd climbed up ladders from room to room, and pretended to be too scared to come down.

A slow grin spread over Tig's face. In some obscure way, he felt happier now.

Right. So it was a mill. And if he could get that trap-door open, he could drop through to the next floor and so on till he got to the bottom where eventually there must be a door. He applied himself again to the wooden trap, but though he pulled and tugged with all his might the wood refused to budge. Tig sat back, momentarily exhausted.

But he was not beaten yet. He looked speculatively at the window. Mills had sails on them, sails like vast ladders. If he could get himself through that window, and on any sort of ledge outside, and from there to one of the sails, he would be able to clamber down to the ground.

Having untied one of his shoes, he took aim at the window. The shoe struck the wooden frame and bounced back: he had to duck to avoid it. He tried again. This time the shoe made contact with the glass. There was a sharp crack, and a long thin line appeared across the pane. Tig went over to collect his shoe. He remembered once, late on a Saturday night, seeing some fool who'd had too much to drink chuck a brick through a plate glass window. They'd had to take him to hospital to put stitches in his face. Tig didn't want that to happen to him. He got hold of some of the sacking which had been his bed, wrapped it round his arm, and then, standing well to the side of the window, his back against the wall, let fly with the shoe.

A satisfying tinkle of glass broke the dusty silence. Tig went to work knocking out the remaining triangles, and then pushed the heap of broken glass up to the wall with his other shoe. He poked his head through the frame.

It had been a good idea — while it lasted. The building stood in a little grassy meadow surrounded by trees and hedges. There was no other building in sight. Nor were there any sails, at least not on this side of the mill. With a grunt Tig turned away in disgust. His eyes fell on the lengths of rope which had bound him. They looked good and thick, a lot thicker than the usual sort of rope you tied trunks with, and Tig remembered once making himself a swing with rope like that suspended from the branch of a tree.

He took another look through the shattered pane. It must be all of thirty feet to the ground, and there were no handy ledges to use as steps. It would have to be the rope. He picked up the sections of rope, trying the strength of them across his chest. They'd have to be tied together, of course. Tig got busy.

He took care over the knots: the ground had looked hard

beneath that window despite the thick wet grass. At last he was satisfied. He looked round for something to tie one end to.

There was nothing. The room was totally bare. He looked up to the beams above his head, but the planks which formed the floor of the next room up fitted tightly, and there was no projection of wood or old nail.

How strong was that window frame? He'd given it a good battering already, but when he pushed it, it seemed firm enough. He inspected it for signs of obvious rottenness. It would have to do. It was a square frame with a two-inch timber dividing it into two from top to bottom. That other pane of glass would have to go, though. He was more practised at it now, and a few seconds' work with the shoe had cleared the frame. He tried the central timber once again, and then tied the knotted rope carefully round it, leaving the rest of the rope dangling through the frame. He looked out. The rope didn't reach the ground, but it was better than nothing. He remembered just in time to put his shoe back on.

Tig got one knee up to the sill, and eased himself onto the frame. It was going to be difficult to get outside — the opening was small and narrow — but now that he'd got as far as this, he had no intention of giving up.

There was one bad moment when he'd got himself outside, his feet on the window-sill, one hand round the central timber of the frame, the other searching for the rope below him. His foot slipped, and he clutched at the wood, praying that it would hold.

He swung by one arm from the frame. He thought he felt it move from its position in the wall, and he wondered briefly what it would be like to hit the ground from this height. Then his other hand found the rope, and he was able, slowly and cautiously, to transfer his weight from the wood.

The rest was easy. Hand over hand he let himself down, kicking himself away from the rough stone of the wall. The rope was too short by ten feet, and he hung to the end of it, getting his breath to jump, when the window-frame saved him the trouble. It snapped with a sound like a pistol, and Tig was on the ground.

He got up, shaking himself all over like a dog emerging from a river. No bones broken, just a bruise or two, and that didn't bother him. He looked round, half-afraid that the people who had put him there might be waiting to put him back again, but the only living creature was a solitary cow which looked at him with melting and incurious eyes. Tig raced for the cover of the trees.

He was in a small plantation of beech and birch. As soon as he had reached its safety, he looked back to see if he was being followed. But nothing stirred. Tig scratched a path in the dry soil at the roots of a tree with the toe of one shoe, as he thought what he should do next. It was strange that he'd been able to escape. Perhaps he was expected to? That supply of food wouldn't have lasted for ever, and if they'd wanted him dead they'd have seen to it before. Perhaps, shortly, they would be coming back? But if that was so, he would be just as dangerous to them as he had been before. He was still confused and uncertain why they should be after him: something he'd seen in the alley, he supposed. It looked as though they just wanted time, as though they wanted him out of the way for a day or so until they had cleared off with whatever it was they had stolen. Or just to frighten him? To keep him quiet? Something about coins from the White Lion Hotel. It must be important to someone, but not so important that he should end up dead for having seen it. Not like that other bloke with the blood on his face.

Tig moved rapidly. He wanted to prove what he thought he knew about the man in the alley, and standing about fidgeting wasn't going to prove anything. The first thing to do was to find out where he was. He ran through the trees.

He came out on a country road, wet and slimy, but completely unoccupied. To Tig, a town boy, the solitude of the countryside was both surprising and unnerving. You couldn't have a road without cars and lorries on it — not a proper road. He began to jog along, hoping for a lift. He didn't know which way to go, but he decided to make south towards the sun. There was something that looked like a sign-post in the distance: it would be a good place to start from.

He had almost reached the sign-post, straining his eyes to read the names on it, when he heard a vehicle behind him. He spun round, shoving his thumb in the air. It was a small van, of a dirty blue colour, and it slowed down as it passed. Tig yelled the name of the town he wanted to go to, and the van-driver shook his head. He said something which Tig didn't catch above the noise of the engine, and made off. After it had disappeared over the brow of the hill, Tig came to the conclusion that the driver had told him he was going the wrong way. He went on to the sign-post and cursed.

Tig began to plod back along the road. There was no point in running: he knew he wouldn't be able to keep it up for eight miles. He must just hope for a lift from some considerate driver, otherwise it was going to take him well over a couple of hours. He glanced at the sun, and was appalled to realise it must be about midday.

It was not a busy road. The light was beginning to fade now, as the mist thickened. He could hear vehicles coming before he could see them, but as far as getting a lift went it seemed that drivers could not see the small thin figure by the roadside with his thumb raised pleadingly. Tig walked on, depressed but determined.

When help came, it was a vast lorry. Tig had heard it, and realising its size he had stepped off the road, but his thumb went up all the same. A round red face looked down at him from the cabin, as the lorry thundered to a halt. Tig scrambled up.

It was warm in the cabin. Tig's spirits began to revive as the heat from the engine penetrated his frame. The lorry-driver talked about dog-racing, but he didn't seem to expect answers.

"Are you going right through?" Tig asked, when he found a long enough pause in the driver's spate of words.

"Right through and out the other side, mate," the driver replied. "Where do you want to be dropped?"

"The High Street'll do."

"Can't stop there. Double yellow lines. I know this place. Them traffic wardens like hawks." The driver lapsed into repetitious profanity. "Tell you what," he went on, "just by the railway bridge, there's a set of traffic lights. I've never yet been through this town without being stopped by them. You can nip out there."

"Thanks."

"You're welcome. What've you been doing, then? On a hike or something?"

"That's right," said Tig. It was easier to agree.

"Stupid," the driver commented. "Man was made for a machine. Clever, that. It means you oughter ride when you can, and let the other jokers walk. Right?"

"I got tired," Tig said.

"You look it, mate, you look it. What did you do? Sleep in your clothes in a ditch?" The driver bellowed with laughter.

Tig looked down at himself. He was covered with mud, some of it from yesterday, but quite a lot from today. And he couldn't care less.

"Traffic lights ahead," the driver announced. "As I thought just turning to red to give me a rousing welcome. Be ready to nip out, youngster."

As the lorry pulled up, Tig scrambled out. He yelled his thanks, but the lorry was making so much noise he doubted whether the driver heard. Tig looked about him with satisfaction.

He saw a police car drawn up in a side-street, and as he watched, the door opened, and a policeman stepped out. He was looking straight at Tig.

Twelve

TIG'S name, age, and general description had been circulated to all patrol-cars in the district shortly after one o'clock. The police had gained the information from the school. They were not much interested in Tig's truancy, but they did want to ask him some more questions about what he had seen in the alley the night the coin collection was stolen from the White Lion Hotel. They realised now that Tig might be able to give them a lead. If his story was to be believed somebody had got at the coins from inside the hotel and dropped them out of the window to two men in the back alley. The boy had seen the men, and it was just possible that he'd seen them clearly enough to furnish a description. So the boy must be found. The message had gone out, and its details were stored more or less exactly in the memories of a score or so patrolmen.

The particular patrolman who saw Tig was lying in wait for traffic offenders at a notoriously bad corner where drivers were known frequently to jump the lights. There had been an accident there only a few days before: a temporary clamp-down had been ordered.

The patrolman's eyes scanned the traffic with fatherly concern. He saw the lorry stop at the red light, and took no more notice until he observed a boy scrambling down from the cab. Dangerous that, he remarked to himself, with traffic all round liable to start up at any moment. He'd better have a word with that boy. He got out of the car and waited for a break in the traffic to cross the road, keeping his eye on the boy all the time. It didn't occur to him that there was anything special about the incident.

Tig stood stock-still for two seconds, unthinking panic beating at his chest. Then he darted off, keeping the traffic between him and the policeman, running low. He heard a roar of command from the other side of the street, but he had no intention of obeying it. He'd told them before, and they hadn't believed him. He had to have proof. And to find that he needed time. He had no spare hours for answering slow and meaningless questions from any copper down at the station.

Tig turned abruptly into a narrow path between two shops, leading to a backyard filled with decrepit sheds. It looked a good place to hide, so long as nobody had seen him come in. Particularly that policeman. He glanced hurriedly round. There was a fence at the back which looked as though it could be climbed. He ran to it and hoisted himself up by way of a pile of wooden boxes. For a moment he looked back to see if there was any sign of pursuit, but all he could see was a large dog which looked at him with friendly eyes. Tig dropped over the fence, then he felt safer. There was no sound of voices raised in anger or command, just the gentle hum of traffic along the main road.

He must somehow get hold of Pete — he'd got tired of playing this all by himself. A quick glance at his watch told him he could probably catch Pete at home just before he went off for afternoon school. There was the business of the sick note, too. Poor old Pete! He must be sweating over that.

Tig made his way by a succession of quiet back roads and alleys to Pete's place. Pete was in the backyard mournfully inspecting his stock of old tyres.

"Where have you been?" he greeted Tig accusingly.

Tig gave him a jaunty "Wotcher!", and then climbed into the hut where he'd spent the night before last. Pete followed him, full of questions.

Tig said, "No time to answer, pal. But I want your help."

"That's all right," Pete grumbled half-heartedly. "You landed me right in it this morning with no sick note."

Tig had the grace to apologise. "But that wasn't my fault, Pete. Honest. Look, I'll tell you. I was out on the common last night with the bike, you know, where the Guy Fawkes bonfire is. And I heard those footsteps again."

"Footsteps!" said Pete, disbelievingly.

"All right, all right, but I did." Tig saw that he'd have to explain everything, so he had a shot at it. Pete looked at him throughout the telling, his eyes wide with incredulity.

"Go on!" he said, when Tig finished.

"You don't believe it," Tig said.

"Course I do, though it seems funny to me. I mean, all for a few old coins. They might have killed you, knocking you on the head like that."

"That's what I didn't understand," Tig went on. "Because if they'd already killed someone else, the bloke in the alley, why didn't they put me out of the way too? And then I thought of the bonfire and the guy. Pete, it does *explain* some things."

"Oh, sure," said Pete. "What are you going to do then?"

"I'm going to find them." Tig spoke with determination.

"Those musicians?"

"Yes."

"You didn't have much luck yesterday."

"I know, but that was because I wasn't looking what I was doing. This time it's going to be different. And I want you to come with me, Pete. Be a pal."

Pete chewed his lower lip.

"What about school?" he said.

Tig told him what he could do with it. "Anyway," he added, "if I'm going to do any forging of sick notes for you, you might as well make it worth my while. One more afternoon won't make any difference. Come on, Pete."

Pete made up his mind. "All right," he said. "I'll come.

Just in case you get your head knocked in again. Not that it wouldn't do you a lot of good."

"Thanks," said Tig briefly.

"I saw Liz a few minutes ago at Rose's. There was something in the *Herald* about a missing paperseller. And Tig, you know the police went round to your place this morning? Your mum came down here to see if we knew where you were, and she told us."

Tig cursed. "It means we've got to work fast, Pete, and keep out of sight. Come on."

They spent the next two hours in an exhausting search through the streets and alleys of the town. The had looked first in the market, and the road where they had previously seen the two musicians, but there was no sign of them there. Tig thought of asking one of the drunks who sat round the fountain in the middle of the market square, but the old man was too far gone to understand what they wanted. He heard the word music, and started singing a spirited rendering of 'Nellie Dean'. In despair they left him.

All the time they kept an eye open for the arm of the law, for Tig had a strong feeling that the police would still be looking for him, particularly after what Pete had told him. Whenever they saw a blue uniform, which happened a number of times, they dived for cover. Pete's lanky form made good camouflage.

By four o'clock they were back in the market square, tired and hungry. The drunks were still at the fountain, though their muttered singing had changed its tune. The stall-holders were beginning to clear up the debris of cardboard boxes and wrappings as the fog thickened and settled over everything. The orange lamps were just managing to cut circles of misty light through the gloom.

"Well?" said Pete, his hands in his pockets.

Tig said nothing. His shoulders showed his discouragement.

"Got any money, Pete?"

"Not much."

"Enough for a couple of hot dogs?"

Pete investigated the contents of his pockets. When they had pooled their resources, they thought they might just do it.

"Harry won't mind," Tig said hopefully.

Harry was there at his usual place in the arcade with his mobile stand. Harry's big red face grinned at them. Custom was brisk.

"He's in a good temper," Tig said to Pete in a low voice. "It doesn't always happen that way. Come on."

Harry greeted them like long-lost brothers.

"You hungry, boys? Help yourself. You're welcome. Roll up, roll up, for the best sizzling hot dogs in town." The last remark was a bellowing roar for the benefit of the whole street.

Pete suddenly had an idea which he communicated to Tig in a whisper. Tig's face cleared. He stopped chewing, half-way through a mouthful, and he looked at Pete in surprise.

"That's not bad!" he mumbled. He finished the mouthful and said, "Harry, have you seen a couple of musicians this afternoon? You know, playing on the streets for money."

"Sure, boy. Why?"

Tig ignored the question.

"Harry, it's important. How long ago?"

"I never knew you was interested in music, kid."

"They friends of yours?"

"Not special."

"Well, your not so special friends are just in the bus-station. Through the arcade, and then into the parking-lot. If you-all weren't making so much noise eating my hot dogs, you'd hear them. They've been there most of the afternoon."

"Thanks, Harry. See you!"

"Be good, kid!"

Tig and Pete walked away through the arcade, keeping

to the side, watching everybody and everything. Half-way down, Tig clutched at Pete's arm.

"Listen!"

The sound of the flute and violin wafted through the foggy atmosphere, sometimes clear, sometimes far-distant. As they walked slowly on, the sounds became easier to distinguish over the clatter of people's feet and the thrumming of their voices.

"It's them," Tig whispered.

They crept quietly through the crowds to the corner of the arcade where it opened out into the tarmacked area of the bus-station.

"What do we do?" Pete wanted to know.

"Dunno," Tig admitted. "Just watch, keep out of sight. And mind where you put your big feet."

The darkness was rapidly gaining now. The buses, looking like great liners on a smooth sea, sailed in and out with the rush-hour traffic. The musicians, over the other side, under the shelter of a chestnut tree, were doing a good trade.

"I can't see why they should want to nick things, when they're making that much profit," Pete complained, after they had stood there some minutes.

"It's good cover," Tig said. They withdrew a bit into the shadow of the arcade. Streams of people bumped into them and whirled round them and swore at them, but they took no notice. "They must be quite well-known about the streets, Pete, so wherever they turned up, nobody much would think it funny. Just those two musicians again, they'd say. Nobody would ever stop them and ask them what they were doing. They could be standing outside a building, any building they liked, for hours, looking for the best place to get in, working out just how to pull the job, and nobody would think of suspecting them. It's clever, Pete."

Pete was thinking. "Yes," he said, "but you said it was two *blokes* you saw in the alley that night when someone threw the case out of the window."

"Well, I thought it was. It was dark, though, too dark to see properly."

Pete pointed with his thumb. "But one of those is a *girl*," he insisted. "Look at all that long hair."

"Well, some blokes do," Tig said defensively.

"Down to the waist?"

"What about a wig?"

Pete was silent for a moment. He peered cautiously round the corner, under the cover of the crowds, to have another look at the violin-player.

"High heels," Pete went on.

"All part of the cover."

"And the scent. You said you recognised the scent she was wearing. Or *he*. A *man*?"

"If you call it after-shave," Tig said.

Pete still looked unbelieving.

"And there's another thing," Tig went on. "I thought it was weird at the time. You remember yesterday when we saw them by the market, and they came after us through the shop?"

"Yeah?"

"Well, just before they saw us, the girl bent down. You know that old cap they have in front of them for people to throw money in. Well, one penny had gone wide. She bent down to pick it up. And that skirt went up at the back. Great big hairy legs, Pete, and the thickest ankles you ever saw. That's no girl."

"I don't see how —" Pete began, when Tig told him to be quiet. They listened. The sounds of the flute and violin were no longer to be heard. Tig poked his head round Pete's shoulder, to get a better look.

"They're packing up," he said, excitement in his voice. "Putting things away. The one with the beard has put the money in his pocket. Come on, Pete. They're off!"

Thirteen

THE two musicians had packed up their instruments, and were walking through the crowds away from the bus-station. Tig and Pete, from behind the cover of a bus, watched them. Tig was reasonably certain he had not been noticed this time, and he had no intention of letting them realise that he was on their tail. Pete was useful here, because be could be seen without being recognised: and he was tall, so that Tig could hide behind him. Pete, who preferred to be led rather than to lead, was reluctant to be pushed into the front, but he had no choice. Tig's insistent urgings, even though Pete had no clear idea what he was meant to be doing, were not to be denied.

Tig himself, if he had stopped to think, would have admitted that he had no real plan of campaign. He would follow them, certainly, but he was leaving the rest to chance. For the moment he had to concentrate on keeping them in sight without awakening suspicion.

In the crowded streets of the rush-hour it was easy. Pete's height gave him an advantage, while Tig peered round people's elbows and occasionally darted into the street to make sure that he hadn't lost sight of them. The musicians, now that their street-entertaining was over, were walking purposefully and fast. Past the ranks of buses they went, and the standing queues of travellers; up by a side-street, into the main shopping-centre of the town.

They turned into one of the the supermarkets, and when Tig realised this he sent Pete in after them in case they went out the back way. He himself moved further up the street to hide himself in the gathering mist. There was a good crowd of people up there. He could use them as shelter.

Tig ran up to the crowd. He was surprised to find they were standing still in a loose circle round a bus in the middle of the road. There was the siren of an ambulance and he could see uniformed policemen. He didn't know what had happened, and he thought it safer to keep out of the way in case some stray policeman spotted him. He tried to listen to what those in front of the crowd were saying.

"Not the driver's fault."

"Can't blame him."

"I never even saw her."

"Just stepped off, she did. Never looked."

"Gor, what a mess!"

"Come on, stand back please. Let the ambulance through."

The crowd, waiting and gaping and craning their heads, parted momentarily as the officials arrived. Tig caught sight of a red plastic carrier bag and somebody's feet sticking out from a blanket. The voices around him were hushed for a second, then natural curiosity took over.

"Don't look too good."

"Dead, is she?"

"Should think so."

"Never stood a chance."

"What a thing to happen."

"Can't be helped."

The crowd parted again. There was a stretcher with two men carrying it; two others, official-looking, by the side. The crowd gathered in again as one of the men looked closely at the bent body.

There was complete silence.

Tig's mind was empty. He heard one of the policemen saying who it was on the stretcher, but it seemed no more than a name. It had sound, but it meant nothing. It had no connection with a living human being. Mrs English, they said it was. Mrs English. Tig made no movement.

The crowd spilled round him. The ambulance was disappearing into the fog now, and people began to disperse, to pick up their lives where they had left them, to go on with their shopping, to think about what they would have for tea. It had been an accident. Such things happen. People die. Somebody else no longer breathing. Sausages, or perhaps a nice pork chop.

Tig was running, long painful strides, his feet tripping in the gutter, his arms pushing into shopping-bags and people's backs. Then he stopped, suddenly, as he came to the department store. Pete was standing outside.

"Quick!" said Pete. "They're coming out."

Tig hid in a shop door with Pete in front of him, their backs to the street. The two musicians came out, passed them. As they did so, a little of a recognisable scent came to Tig's nostrils, and with that came memory.

His mind was no longer empty. It was full of anger, a burning white-hot rage. He had promised his mother he would go to school and he had broken that promise. He couldn't help that — it wasn't his fault. But now there came to him the realisation that he would never be able to explain to her why he had not done what he had said he would do.

It was an anger so huge, so monstrous, that it left no space for anything else, an anger which allowed one easement only. Tig knew who had hit him and bound him and taken him away. Tig knew who had prevented him going to school. Tig knew who was going to answer for it. He had to blame *somebody*.

"You all right?" Pete said.

Tig shook himself free from thought.

He nodded.

"You'd gone all white."

"I'm OK."

"Sure?"

"Sure. Which way did they go?"

"Up the High Street. We'd better be quick."

Still with caution they trailed after the two musicians. They had not far to go. The two in front took a turning off the High Street and entered the network of narrow lanes behind. It was now more difficult for Tig and Pete to follow without being seen. The streets were short, devoid of useful cover, and they ended almost invariably with a cross-roads. A few minutes of this however took them beyond the older quarter of the town towards the common.

"Where are they going?" Pete wanted to know.

Tig did not reply. His face was set, and his mind was still full of anger, though it had now become cold and calculating rather than passionate.

There was a lane which led away by the side of the common towards the open countryside. Little cottages and old ramshackle farm buildings lined one side; the other was clear of building, and stretched into the blackness of the old golf-course. Somewhere there was a pyramid of wood for the bonfire.

The two musicians turned off the lane and disappeared between two groups of cottages. From the shelter of a straggling hawthorn hedge, Tig saw them disappear into the maze of sheds and out-houses at the back. He strained his eyes to see just where they were, but the darkness had swallowed them. There were no lights in the windows. The roofs of the sheds were a jagged black line against the fog.

Pete started to say something, but Tig grabbed his arm. "Shut up!" he whispered urgently. "Listen."

There was no sound from the houses round about. If they were inhabited, they kept their miserly secrets well. But Tig could hear the crunch of the man's shoes on loose gravel, and the shorter sharper click of the one who wore high heels. There was the squeak of wood as a door opened, and a muffled bang as it shut. A square of window sprang into life, sending a beam of light through the fog across the gravel path. Tig and Pete cowered back to the lee of the hedge. Then a curtain was pulled across the window, leaving an outline of dirty yellow. Tig heard someone laugh.

With boundless care he moved out from the shadows. He could hear Pete moving behind him, and he stopped.

"You stay here."

"Why?"

"Just stay."

Pete moved back. Tig waited until he could hear no sound, and then tried his feet on the path. That flash of light from the window had revealed a darker edge to the gravel, which he hoped was grass. He put a hand down to feel, and expelled a light sigh of satisfaction as he found it was. He stepped over the gravel and pressed himself to the wall of the cottage on his right. All the time his eyes were on the square outline at the end of the alley. He was ready at a moment to freeze against the wall.

He worked his way with slow care down the side of the cottage. At one time his foot touched what felt like a bottle, which tipped over and fell with a soft bounce on the grass. Tig held his breath as he stopped it rolling onto the gravel with his heel. It stayed still. Tig moved on.

It was a large wooden building at the end of the alley. It might have been a coach-house or stables at some time in the past, when it mattered to someone. Now it was old, and twisted. Tig could feel the drops of dry tar along the planks. He let his fingers pass over them almost lovingly. The window was set high in the wall, too high for him to get his eyes to the level of the sill unless he could find something to stand on. He hoped for a box or a log of wood, but nothing was visible in the smoky darkness.

It was then for the first time that Tig noticed the smoke. It was like a distant bonfire, hanging in the air and giving it a taste as well as a smell. Tig remembered the bonfire in the middle of the common. One rocket, the first of the evening, exploded in a rain of red and yellow and green somewhere away in the distance above the fog.

Tig stood on his toes under the window, and his fingers clutched at the wooden frame. His legs kicked, involuntarily, as he tried to lever himself up, and his toe scraped the boards. He was still.

It was a good stout window-sill. Tig found that with a controlled effort he could raise himself by his arms until his eyes were level with the bottom of the window. He hoped desperately for a tear or a gap in the curtain. He held his body stiff, taking his weight entirely on his hands. He had about three seconds before his muscles rebelled, and he found himself forced to lower his body gently to the ground. But he had seen, and the picture remained printed in his memory.

The two musicians were sitting at a bare wooden table in a room furnished with dusty boxes and crates. There was a low brown sink in one corner with a rusty tap. An aged dirty sofa stood against one wall, its stuffing oozing out from torn covers. A circular paraffin fire smoked and glimmered by the table.

The violin-player had lost his long straight hair and his trailing skirt, and wore faded jeans. His face was young and pink, and his eyes gleamed in the light of a naked bulb hanging from the rafters above the table. He was counting coins, piling them up to a regular height. The flute-player with the beard watched him from the other side of the table.

But Tig wanted more than this. What he had seen on the table was the proceeds of their street-entertainment. But if these men were really the two he had seen, however fleetingly, in the lane behind the White Lion, they must have other coins hidden somewhere. Otherwise, nothing made sense. There *had* to be a reason for that leather case thrown through the window. Even more, there *had* to be a reason for his own capture and imprisonment.

Tig felt around with his foot. He found a stone, large and jagged, and he picked it up, testing it in his hand. He lobbed the stone up into the air so that it curved over the roof of the building. It fell on the tiles with a satisfying crash.

There was a moment's silence. Then the door burst open. Two black figures leapt out, but they did not see Tig crouching in the darkness of the wall. They ran past him and round the corner of the shed.

"You OK, Tig?" came the sound of Pete's voice from the hedgerow. Tig silently cursed. He could hear the men stop, then run back. They must have heard Pete's shout. He had no time to waste. He slipped quietly inside. With another part of his brain, as though it was outside himself, he knew that the men would be coming through the door in no more than a second or two. His eyes darted round looking for a place to hide. Why couldn't Pete keep quiet? He slid behind a pile of crates in the most shadowy corner.

He was not aware of the reappearance of the musicians until his nose caught that faint scent he had recognised before. They were very quiet, and clearly suspicious. The door closed with hardly a sound. A slight scrape of a box on the wooden floor told Tig that they had returned to the table in the middle of the room.

"Cats?" The voice was soft and smooth. Tig guessed that it belonged to the younger of the two.

"I don't know." Tig could feel the bearded man's eyes searching the corners and the shadows. "There was somebody shouting the name Tig."

"That English boy?"

"I'll give him French and English if I catch him again. We were too soft. It doesn't pay. We should have finished him properly when we had him. One more wouldn't have made all that difference."

"One more?"

"You know what I mean. Putting him out of the way for a day or two was your idea. Soft as usual."

"But the money." Still the same soft whine.

"It's safe enough."

"Are you sure? The door was open."

"You've got an obsession with those coins, haven't you? Another day and we'll be rid of them. You've got to be patient."

"But they might have gone."

The bearded man grunted. There was another scrape of wood. Tig, in his dark corner, took a chance. If the man was getting up from the table, and turning round, he might not notice a movement behind him in the corner. Tig slowly raised his head above the edge of the crate which sheltered him. The bearded man was burrowing in a bucket of what looked like sand under the sink. It was a red bucket with the word 'Fire' painted on its side in large black letters. The younger man's eyes followed every movement greedily.

The bearded man growled a curse, stood up, turned, and slapped an iron box on the table. It was a plain affair, heavy, solid, about the size of a thick book. The young man's hands went out to it. The other man pushed him away. He raised his eyes to glare at him, and his gaze found Tig.

There was a second's shocked and appalling silence. Tig leapt. He had no conscious plan. All he wanted to do was to get out. He ran for the door. The young man half-rose from his chair at the commotion behind him, and for one precious moment hid Tig from view. And into Tig's mind there came an odd and silly idea.

A wooden crate was close to his hand. He swerved, threw the crate with all his might at the great gaping bearded mouth in front of him, and with the same action seized the iron box. He heard a roar, and a splintering crash, and he felt something hit his shoulder. He sprang for the door. He could feel the misty air cold on his face. He sprinted as he had never known he could.

"Run for it, Pete!" he yelled. *"Run!"*

Fourteen

TIG ran with the iron box clutched tight to his chest. He was on the common. Fog covered the whole area of little hills and valleys, making the night blacker and the paths harder to find. Ahead of him a dull red glow spread through the damp air.

Tig's breath came in great gasps, his legs felt as heavy as though they were made of the same metal as the box he held, his head seemed curiously light. He was aware of footsteps behind him, and for a moment despair gripped him. He tripped on a hillock of grass, his knees gave, and he found his mouth full of wet grass. He lay in a shallow ditch at the roots of a thorn tree, panting.

The footsteps, thudding and sliding on the wet surface of the path, pounded nearer. He heard his name called. With a searing expulsion of breath he yelled back, "Pete!"

Pete's lengthy body cut through the fog. He pulled himself to a stop, gazing searchingly ahead. Tig dragged his arms from the mud and put his weight on his knees. He gave a low whistle.

"Tig! Where are you?"

"Here, you fool."

Pete blundered against the prickly branches of the tree and swore. Tig laughed: the arrival of Pete had sent his panic flying. His head throbbed, but that, he realised, was lack of food more than anything else. He pulled Pete down into the shadows. His ears strained to catch the sound of pursuing feet.

There was a noise of crackling and burning, and it took Tig a moment or two to understand its significance. Then suddenly the sky was blood-red, as the flames leapt from the bonfire. There was a smell of petrol in the air. They could hear the excited voices of children, the shouts of men, and the small irregular explosions of jumping crackers. Two great rockets split the darkness with a rush of yellow rain.

Tig got up, mechanically brushing his knees.

"They're not following," he said. He sounded puzzled.

"Sure?" Pete said, as he scrambled from the ditch.

"Course not. But they haven't come, have they?"

"What did you see there, Tig?"

"Nothing much." It was too complicated to explain. And anyway, he felt tired. The glow of the fire attracted him with its warmth and sense of safety. There were people standing round. Lots of people. Safety in numbers.

Tig remembered a face, cold, white, with streaks of blood, and staring eyes. He remembered a grotesque shape in a pram with a scarf tied round its head and a red-nosed mask over its face. He broke into a run. Pete loped along behind.

"What you doing, Tig?"

Tig saved his breath for running. When he came nearer he could feel the warmth of the other people, the sense of security which being part of a large number gives to a single individual. He could melt into this multitude, become part of it, live as a member of it, forget his fear. He knew what he was afraid of — not flying footsteps behind him or hands held out to grasp him, not the possibility of physical pain, nor even loss of his own existence. He was afraid of being alone. Alone with himself. He was, and now for the first time the realisation of it bit into his mind, without somewhere to go; he was an unnoticed island in a sea of huge and unknowable proportions. The fire was a home; the people round it, for the time being, friends.

He held out his hands to the blaze. The iron box was in his way, and he almost threw it down. Then memory came back to him, and with it that same cold anger which he had felt before. It would take a very big fire to melt the ice of that anger.

He turned his face to the top of the huge pyramid. The flames, leaping and dancing on the petrol-soaked wood, seemed to be trying to reach the stars whose little light twinkled ineffectively on the blanket of mist. They were joyous flames, glad and comforting. Tig felt in himself something that was almost a longing to be part of them. He moved nearer till the heat at the base of the pyramid scorched his legs. It was as though he could hear a voice inside the fire calling him. He wanted to answer it.

Pete caught hold of his arm, and Tig tried to shake him off.

"Leave go of me!" he shouted but his words were directed as much to the joyful flames as to Pete.

A man with a gardening fork whose job seemed to be to tend the fire clumped towards him.

"Come on, lad. You're too near there. You'll get yourself burnt. Let somebody else see a bit of the fire."

The calm and cheerful voice brought Tig to his senses. He slapped a hand against his jeans, and jumped away.

"Mind where you're going."

"Look out, can't you?"

"Who do you think you are?"

Shouts and whistles all round him. The crowd which before had been so comforting broke into individual pieces, some amused, some irritated, some blustering and officious.

Tig moved further away. Pete hovered by his side.

There was a stand a little distance away, roped off to keep small children out of the way. Here two or three men in shirt sleeves set matches to fireworks as fast as they could. Rockets rose into the air, wheels spun, and candles popped and sputtered. Tig and Pete stood watching, with the crowd round them.

But while he watched, something nagged at the back of Tig's mind. He knew there was something important he had to do, important to *him*. He turned back to the fire and forced himself to look up to the top of the mighty pile. The orange flames had reached the summit now; they were leaping in free abandon into the empty night. And in their dazzling glare the figure of Guy Fawkes showed white and insubstantial. His boots, large black boxes, smouldered. Red tongues jerked about his jacket and reached up to the coloured scarf and the comic mask, which, as Tig watched in horror, melted into nothingness. A loud cheer rose from the crowd.

Red fire and red scarf mingled together. The whole figure burst into sudden soaring flame. Pieces of straw like sparks flew upwards as the body fell to bits and collapsed in on itself. For a moment the wooden framework stood out gaunt and black against the roaring hissing blaze, until that too slipped down into the heart of the pyramid with a quick explosion of sparks. The glowing timbers settled round it, creaking and grating.

Tig stared in wonder. The fear that had been in the back of his mind melted as he had seen the straw stuffing melt. He knew what he had expected to see when the red and white scarf disintegrated, and there had been nothing there.

He had been wrong, and he was glad.

He watched the flaming pyramid and the whirring and exploding fireworks with contentment. Pete was saying something to him, but his words were lost in the general noise, and in any case Tig did not want to listen. Pete had begun to shout, and Tig shouted as well, wild roaring meaningless hoots and yells, for no better reason than that he wanted to blot out the memory of his fear. Others round him began to sing and howl. Noise rose like the sparks of the fire. A little breeze stirred the hot timbers, bringing smoke down in whirling columns and solid masses. People played and danced through it. They rubbed their eyes as the smoke poured after them, clogging their noses and making them splutter. It was a race between people and smoke, and Tig was out in front leading the mob. There were footsteps behind him, friendly stampeding footsteps now, but he knew he could beat them. Others he met found themselves drawn into the endless swirling circle. Round and round the fire they went till they fell exhausted on the wet grass. Then they sat and stared into the flames, mouths open, eyes bright.

A man with a shovel began to explore the edges of the fire, searching for potatoes. He swore and muttered to himself as the heat burned his face and the sparks landed on his fingers. Potatoes, charred and black, rolled out to the waiting circle. Hands grabbed and juggled.

Tig sat quietly warming his fingers round the rough skin of the half-cooked potato which had landed at his feet. He looked round for Pete, but Pete seemed to have gone. He called out to him. Round the other side, he supposed.

It was in the stillness after the storm of noise that Tig sensed someone behind him. His fingers gripped the potato, though he knew somewhere in the back of his mind that the skin of his palms was scorched.

A change of air, a puff of smoke, and after it a scent. Tig knew that scent. At once all his senses, all his mind, told him he must run. But there was one other thing he must do first. The iron box which he had carried with him all the time he had been circling the fire was now by his feet. As the smoke swirled round him, blotting out the light, he took the box in his hand and hurled it as far as he could. It flew into the air, glittering in the flames, and then it fell, and as it fell, Tig was on his feet and was away.

Through the crowds he ran, into the fog and the darkness, away from the red fire, to find the shelter of the night. He had no idea which direction he took, and it surprised him when he found himself at the stile where he had left his bike the night before. Something gleamed wet in the mist. He grabbed the handlebars, his only emotion one of astonishment that it should still be there. It was old and battered, but it was the only solid possession left to him.

Tig swung the bike round. He could hear the boots of the men thudding on the path. He smiled a little as he jumped on the saddle. He was going to enjoy himself.

The gradient of the path gave him extra speed as he pedalled with all his strength at the two shadowy figures approaching through the mist. He shouted as he aimed himself deliberately at them, and he shouted again in triumph when they scattered before him, one to each side. His one regret was that he had not hit them.

The bike carried him on at a roaring speed. He stood up on the pedals, and looked back for any sign of pursuit, but the two figures had faded away, nor was there any sound of their feet. He laughed aloud.

Ahead was the red glow of the fire. He wondered whether to return there, to find Pete, just to be part again of that glorious mob. But that was all over. The fear he had known was burning in the red heart of the fire, and now he was free of it.

He turned away and rode along a path which crossed the common diagonally and led to the river. Tig had always liked this stretch of the river. It was not wide, little more than a deep stream, taking its burden of spring water down to the main river at the other end of the town. But it was a friendly stream with a companionable gurgling ripple over a shallow bed of gravel.

Tig dumped his bike at the edge. He was looking for a particular willow tree whose branches hung in festoons of thin spidery rods and dangled their ends in the water. It was a good place to sit with your back against the gnarled trunk, and your feet stretched out towards the stream.

The mist hung gently over the water as Tig found his tree and settled down at its roots. His eyes roamed lazily over the changing silvery path of the stream, and he wondered where the light came from. The water seemed to have its own sheen, dim and ghostly, but still strangely revealing. The black shapes of trees and bushes gradually became clearer as Tig's eyes grew accustomed to the hazy light. Mist moved and swelled like some live creature.

Tig did not know how long he sat there. Pictures formed in the mist and in the water and the pictures filled his mind. Words breathed in the moving air. A sort of pattern began to become clear, as though he were cleaning mud from his bike to reveal the name of the maker.

Names. They were the things that puzzled him now. The more he thought, the more he knew that there was only one answer to the problem of the names. He felt betrayed.

The cold air bit through his clothes. He shivered and changed his position. He supposed he would have to go. But still he stayed at the roots of the willow tree, watching the changing patterns on the stream's dim surface. Without thinking of it, he would have been happy to stay there all night with the chattering of the water and the movement of the willow branches for company.

The bank on which he sat was straight, but further down-stream the water became shallower and wider. A little bay had eaten into the grass, and there the gravel shone palely in the mist. At the further end of the bay, the water swirled round some black shadowy obstruction.

Tig's eyes were drawn in the direction of the little bay. He was intrigued by the shape round which the water gurgled. He stretched his thin body, his arms above his head. His mouth opened in a contented yawn. He got up because he wanted to feel his legs moving again. He thought he would kick loose the log or whatever it was in the stream, and watch it sail off into the night. Pushing his head through the curtain of willow branches, he ambled along the bank.

It was not a log which obstructed the quiet efficiency of the current.

Tig stared down. He saw a face, and a little body. The strange quiet movement of the water had set it free from the heavy weights which for a time had held it pinned to the bed of the stream. Now it floated loose, uncertain. The face was no longer streaked with blood, as before Tig had seen it. It was washed clean now and it shone innocently in the pale shadows.

Fifteen

INSPECTOR Roberts looked bleakly at the yellow lamps in the street outside his office window. It was late, and he wished he wasn't there. If only he'd decided to accept that invitation to play bridge, coveniently forgetting to tell anyone the telephone number, he wouldn't have been dragged back here in the middle of a filthy night to attend to a body discovered in a stream. Well, Steadman was out there now with the van and the photographers. He ought to be reporting back soon. No point in fussing until he knew the facts. Roberts watched the fog drifting along the empty street.

It was some time before Steadman put in an appearance. When he came, he looked tired. His face was thin and drawn, and a light covering of droplets of fog on his eyebrows and hair made him look greyer.

"There's no doubt about it, sir."

Roberts turned and waited.

"It's the little bloke from the paper-stand all right. The doc says he's been dead for two days or so — it fits with the night of the Hotel robbery — beaten about the head with great chunks of wood. Multiple injuries."

"Funny he wasn't found till this evening," Roberts remarked thoughtfully. "Plenty of people must go that way. There's a tow-path, and houses not all that far away. How did he get there? He didn't throw himself in the stream, now did he? Footprints on the bank?"

"Hundreds," said Steadman briefly. "We've got flashlight photographs, but I doubt if they'll be much use. Looked like bicycle wheels as well."

"You can't carry a body on the cross-bar," Roberts commented. "Who found him anyway?"

"That's the odd thing, sir. That boy."

"Boy? The French kid?"

"John English, sir."

"That's the chap. You've got him then."

"Yes, sir. I've put him in the canteen with a cup of tea and a nice motherly woman PC. I warned her she might have to sprint if he made a break for it."

"Better lock the door as well," Roberts grunted. "Has he talked?"

"Not much, sir."

"Let's have him up then."

"I'd suggest you left him for a bit, sir. He's said a bit, but he looks about done in. His mother was the woman under the bus this afternoon."

"Good Lord, I'd forgotten that. Does he know?"

"Yes, sir. Apparently he saw her being taken away in the ambulance."

"How's he taken it? Shocked?"

"Difficult to say, sir. He's one of those silent kids. I think he's got the idea he's tough, like so many of these kids at that age, but it's only a sort of skin, sir, and not a very thick one either."

"But he's being looked after?"

"He's getting outside a good healthy meal, sir. Gives him something to do."

Roberts scowled at his desk.

"So we've got a murder on our hands," he said heavily.

"*Might* be an accident, sir. The doc wasn't too sure after a cursory examination. Knocked down by a car, perhaps, and just left."

"You said something about wood."

"Fragments of wood found in the hair, sir, but they could have got there afterwards."

"H'm. Not so likely, Jack."

"I agree, sir."

"The point is, is this connected with the hotel robbery, or is it totally separate? That's where this boy's evidence is going to be important. A few words can't hurt, Jack. Let's go down to the canteen and see him. I could do with a cup of tea myself."

They found Tig finishing a large plate of eggs, beans, and chips. The W.P.C. who sat opposite him with her hands round a steaming mug made to get up when she saw Roberts, but he waved her down. He and Steadman fetched themselves mugs of tea and brought up a couple of extra chairs.

"It's a filthy night," Roberts began conversationally.

Tig went on shovelling beans into his mouth.

"I'm sorry about your mother, lad."

Tig glared. What had it got to do with them? If they'd only listened the first time, things might have been different . . .

Roberts was puzzled by the cold anger in Tig's eyes. He stirred his tea slowly with a plastic spoon.

"You were just walking along the stream, then?"

"What of it?" Tig shouted. He was startled by the sound of his own voice, and his eyes fell on the almost empty plate in front of him.

"Nothing, lad, nothing. And you just happened to notice this body."

Tig nodded. He didn't want to say anything. He had a horrible feeling that if he said a single word, he would cry. He could feel the pricking at the corners of his eyes. He concentrated on the plate.

"How long had you been there, by the stream?"

"Dunno." It was more of a growl than human speech.

"Where were you going, lad?"

Tig moved his shoulders. How would he know?

Roberts sighed into his tea and nodded at Steadman.

"Two nights ago," Steadman said very quietly, as though he was talking to himself, "you were in the alley by the side of the White Lion Hotel. It was about seven o'clock, foggy and dark. You saw two people on the pathway beneath a window, and someone inside passing the case out to the other two. Did you see the person inside at all? No, I suppose not. Any light would have been behind him, and you'd have seen just an outline."

Steadman paused a moment, thinking back to the reports he had read.

"They had a torch, didn't they? A beam of light flashed round, and it caught their faces. You'd recognise them again, I reckon."

Tig shifted. "I did recognise them," he said.

"Ah." Steadman glanced up briefly, then his eyes returned to the mug of tea.

"Somewhere in the town, eh? Where now, I wonder?"

The silence was broken by the ticking of the clock on the wall.

"Well, it's a big town, and plenty of people in it. A man with a beard, and another one. That right?"

"It was two men. I thought one of them was a woman, but it isn't."

"I see." Steadman continued to talk to his tea. The boy was beginning to gain confidence. "So there were two men on the pavement, though one might have been a woman, and there was someone else up at the window. But that wasn't all. There was somebody lying in the gutter. A little man. A midget."

Tig pushed the plate violently away. His hand went to the mug in front of him and closed round it.

"I thought he was dead," he said.

"And you came round to the station and reported it, and then a constable went to look, and found nothing."

"They didn't believe me." Tig's voice was flat.

"Just thought you were having them on, I expect.

Natural enough. But it was true, all right. There *was* a body and it disappeared, and it turned up again in the stream tonight."

Tig gripped the mug with tense fingers.

"I think you know all about it, John," Steadman suggested quietly.

"No!" Tig shouted, but he still looked at the mug.

"Strange it was you who found it both times," Steadman said. "It's almost as though you knew where to look."

The silence seemed interminable. Tig's hands were taut and white, his shoulders rigid.

Inspector Roberts had listened to Steadman's questions, as he had often listened before. They worked as a team, and there usually came a point in Steadman's quiet insistent sentences when Roberts fired an unexpected shot. He did so now. It was a chance, but it might work.

"Did you kill him?"

The syllables, dry and brittle, fell into the silence. Tig's head shot up, but he said nothing. His mind was too full of fury for his tongue to frame the right words. None of the swear words he knew seemed strong enough to express what he felt. But his eyes were bright with anger, and his fists were clenched.

Roberts was satisfied. It wasn't clean, but the boy's reserve had to be broken somehow. All he had to do was wait.

Five seconds ticked away, while Tig glared at Roberts.

"I didn't!" Tig's voice rose. "You can't pin it on me! You don't know anything. You don't even know where they live."

"And you do?" Steadman said, still quietly.

"Course I do."

"Then you'll take us there." It was a fact, not a question.

Tig's shoulders relaxed. "Sure," he said. "Why not?"

Roberts sighed. "Let's go."

Two police cars swept without fuss through the town. Steadman drove the first one, with Tig in the back by the side of Inspector Roberts. Two or three more officers followed in the second car. They came to the end of the lane which stretched along one side of the common, and there they came to a halt, their lights and engines off. Silently, they got out.

"How far down, lad?" Steadman's quiet friendly voice came to Tig's ears.

Tig pointed. "Not far."

Feet fell lightly on the wet surface of the road, a soft padding in the smoky air. The dull glow of the remains of the bonfire faintly painted the fog. Tig led them to the black mouth of the alley between the houses. A little ribbon of light from the window of the wooden building at the back showed its occupation. Tig was told to stay by the hedge out of the way. He was amused to notice that one police officer stayed with him, and was surprised by his own amusement. Was he supposed to be so much in danger that he had to have a police escort? But he'd already been inside that building once that evening. He was rather proud of that. They ought to be grateful for his help. They'd never have got there at all if it hadn't been for him.

Tig didn't know what he expected to happen. Half an hour before he would have said that there was only one thing he wanted just then, to be allowed to go away somewhere quietly and sleep. But now he was awake. Perhaps it was the effect of all those baked beans. The chips had been good and crisp, too.

Tig waited. He hoped for a bit of excitement. But the expected explosion of energy was like a firework left in the rain. He heard a knock at the door, a polite friendly knock. He strained his senses to catch any sound or sight from the wooden building. He could imagine the momentary silence inside, the anxious glance, the hurried movement, the attempt to make the place look respectable and non-committal.

The door opened. A few words. A slam of wood, and a kick. A scuffle, nothing more — they might have been just play-acting, it looked so unreal. Two figures outlined in the light streaming from the open door, one dark and bearded, the other young and pink. They walked each between two others. Their feet scrunched on the gravel. The thud of car doors. Lights on, engine revving. A sweep of head-lights, as the car circled. Silence.

Nothing else.

Inspector Roberts called from the door of the building. Tig and the policeman who had been left to guard the alley-mouth moved out of the shadows and went to the lighted doorway. Roberts was standing in the middle by the table, Steadman was picking up the boxes and chairs and putting things to rights.

"Quite like an old-fashioned thieves' kitchen," Steadman remarked. "Nicely out of the way, rent paid in advance, what more do you want?"

Roberts grunted. "All very well, Jack. We can hold them for resisting arrest, but it would be nice to have a bit more evidence." His eyes roved round the bleak dirty room. He walked to the door in the far wall and flung it open. His torch-beam cut into the darkness.

"H'm. Just another shed. Boxes. Have to give it a thorough going-over tomorrow. Pity."

"I agree, sir," Steadman said, "It would be nice to have something more definite."

Tig laughed inside himself. He wasn't going to show them that he was laughing, because that would spoil it. He sucked his cheeks in to stop the laughter bubbling over into a grin. There was something he *could* do, though.

Tig marched to the sink. It was a chance, it might not work, but it was worth taking. He picked up the red bucket marked 'Fire' and hauled it over to the table. Without a word he up-ended it and allowed the coarse sand to spill out over the table-top.

"What the blazes . . ." Roberts began.

Tig smoothed down the heap of sand. His fingers located odd little patches of hardness. He brushed the sand away, and stood back. He was pleased with himself — it had worked.

There were five small leather purses lying on the table, each not much bigger than a match-box. Roberts opened one and tipped it upside-down. Something bright sparkled in the light-brown sand.

"Well, I'm damned!" Roberts exclaimed. "Recognise that, Jack?"

"Part of the haul from Ainstone House, a fortnight back, sir."

"That's right. We ought to be able to clear up a number of outstanding little matters with this lot. It was a good thing we came, Jack. An excellent evening's work." He sounded like a schoolmaster congratulating himself on a pupil's work.

Roberts explored the insides of the others purses, while Steadman and the constable looked on.

"Pity no coins," Roberts said regretfully. "Probably here somewhere. We'll leave a guard tonight, and get the whole place cleaned out when it's light. We'll have to do something about that boy for tonight. Should be some neighbours who'd take him in for the time being. Know anyone along your street, lad? Hey, Steadman! Where *is* that damned boy?"

But Tig was not there.

Sixteen

THE sixth of November saw a lightening of the fog. A watery sun tried to push through the atmosphere, though there was no strength in it. Pete lumbered down the back yard of his house to the shed at the bottom of the garden. His collection of old tyres was growing steadily. Pete was proud of it, though his parents frequently told him it was about time that mess in the corner got cleared up. But it was going to be worth money, that mess, if he could only find the right buyer. He came down most mornings to inspect his assets.

Pete was leaning his long body against a pile of tyres and watching the sun play games with fragments of mist, when he became aware of a disturbance behind him. The cat, he thought, and took no more notice. The cat was a tabby, an engaging creature, about a year old, but it did have the habit of demanding attention, more like a dog than a cat, Pete sometimes thought, but without the dog's sense of obedience.

The scratching noises continued.

"Come out of it!" Pete yelled, without bothering to look.

"All right, I'm coming."

Pete whirled round. Tig's sleepy face peered out from the half-open door of the shed.

"Tig! What the hell are you doing?"

"Getting up," Tig said reasonably. "It's about time."

Pete stared at him in wonder. "You making a habit of this?" he asked.

"Could do worse, mate. Not exactly posh, but it'll do." Tig stretched luxuriously. "Where did you get to last night?"

"I looked for you, but I thought you'd gone, so I came home. Say, Tig, what happened?"

Tig stared at a broken flower-pot. "Nothing much."

"Aw, come on, Tig!" Pete sounded disgusted.

"The police got the two," Tig said reluctantly.

"The musicians?"

"Spot on, mate. And there was a body in the stream."

Pete's eyes opened wide. "Go on!"

"It's true."

"What did you do?"

"Told the police. They went and got it out. It was that little fellow I saw in the alley. Remember? They said he used to sell papers by the hotel, you known that wooden hut? I remember him being there, but I never knew he was a midget."

"Nor did I."

"That's all."

"But how did he get there? And who killed him?"

"Search me." Tig shrugged. He stepped over the piles of tyres, and scratched his head.

"You look a mess," Pete said critically.

"You're no beauty yourself. Got a comb?"

"Inside."

"Oh. Pete, that body. I've got an idea about that, about who killed him. About a lot of things, though there's some more I want to find out."

"So you're not going to school then?"

Tig grinned. "That's what you think, pal. I nipped off last night from the coppers when I got fed up with them. I wanted a bit of freedom to sort things out. They'll be looking for me. Stupid questions. And they never listen when you tell 'em." Tig's voice rose in scorn. "Well, the one place they won't think of looking will be the school, so that's where I'm going to be. You've got to play it clever, Pete."

Pete looked worried.

"But you won't have a note," he objected. "There'll be a lot of fuss. And there's my note for the other day too. But you can write one for yourself, Tig? And me?"

Tig's shoulders collapsed. He pushed his hands into the depths of his pockets. and stared at nothing.

"There's always a fuss," he muttered. He kicked a stone viciously against the fence, and was glad when it hit a jam jar and broke it. He *could* tell Pete, he supposed, about the accident yesterday afternoon, but he didn't want to remember it. His mind went empty when he thought of it, and that was the way he wanted it to be. Why couldn't people mind their own business? A bus ran somebody over, that was all.

"Any chance of breakfast?" he said.

"Sure thing, Tig. Look, you'd better come on in. Mum won't mind."

Pete's mother was small and busy. She looked over her shoulder as Pete's frame filled the door. She was doing things at the cooker with a frying-pan.

"Nearly ready," she said. "Sit down, Peter. Who's that?"

"It's Tig."

Tig sidled in and looked sheepish.

"Well, don't stand there letting the cold air in. Sit down, the pair of you. No, you don't, though, young Tig. You'll find a bar of soap and a towel by the sink. Use 'em. You look as though you've been sleeping in a coal-shed!"

Tig went to the sink and unwillingly washed his face and hands. To his surprise he felt better for it. Pete's mother eyed him shrewdly.

"I suppose it's nothing to do with me," she began. Tig clutched a knife and fork and prayed that she would be quiet.

"Thanks," he said, hoping to stop her.

"I know what you're thinking, Tig," she went on. "And I was told last night. I'm sorry, and I shan't say any more about it. Except that she won't be fit for visitors tonight. I'll take you round tomorrow, if you like."

Tig said nothing. His mind was in a whirl. He'd thought his mother was dead, but he should have known better. It'd take more than a bus to beat his mum. He stared at the plate in front of him, not daring to look up.

"I told them you can stay here, and welcome, for a bit," she went on. "Peter will just have to take up less room, that's all. Have you got any money for your dinner?"

Tig shook his head.

"Well, that won't break me." She found her purse in a drawer, and brought out the necessary change. "Enough for the two of you."

"Thanks," Tig muttered.

"Don't just sit there. You're letting it get cold."

Tig started eating, and discovered how hungry he was. Pete had been tucking in for some minutes. His mother watched them in silence, though she seemed to be busy at the sink.

"Bring the plates over here," she said at length. "That's right. Time to go, or you'll be late."

"Thanks," Tig muttered again. He made his escape, and managed to whistle as he went down the back yard. He had an idea growing at the back of his mind, and he wanted to turn it over. He said little on the way to school. Pete loped along in companionable silence. He was used to it.

Tig was right — there *was* a fuss. He was sent for by a number of people and talked to, but there it ended. Nothing else. Not even told not to do it again. And then he realised the reason for their apparent kindness, and he became angry. He was short, abrupt, and impertinent: the idea of anyone being sorry for him was a novel one, and one that he found difficult to take. Authority sighed over him and let him go.

He sat at the back of the class, and if anyone pitied him enough to leave him alone, he was glad of the time to think. He wondered *why* he'd got so upset about the body in the stream. He remembered the face as he had first seen it, streaked with dirt and blood, in the yellow beam of torchlight in the alley. He remembered it clean and washed by the stream when he next saw it.

The poor little bloke had looked helpless. He was so small, when you saw him outside the covering shelter of the wooden shed where he'd sold his papers. He must have liked that, being hidden so that people didn't know that beneath his head and shoulders little legs swung far from the ground. If they'd known, people would have picked on him too, just for being small. Tig supposed that was why he himself felt involved in what had happened to the paper-seller.

Somebody, or perhaps several, had come up to him and round him as he went down that dark alley, and they'd beaten him with bits of wood till he was dead. They may not have meant to kill him, just rob him probably, and beat him enough to stop him following them to get the money back. But they'd beaten him to death all the same. Or someone else had later on, perhaps? It didn't make any difference to the paper-seller that they hadn't meant to.

The business of the classroom went on round him, but Tig took little notice. The time came for dinner, and he and Pete went in and had it together and moaned about the food as usual, the customary mechanical words that concealed thought but did not prevent it. Pete wanted to know why the police were so interested in what Tig had to say, and when they'd come to take him away. It made Tig laugh aloud to think that they were probably out combing the town for him, and there he was being a good boy at school. Well, it was a fair imitation.

"What's there to laugh at?" Pete demanded. "It's this meatless meat again."

"Like the one about the bishop and the actress," said

Tig, but Pete just looked puzzled.

During the afternoon Tig was busy trying to work things out.

The pram. And the Guy Fawkes in it. For two days they'd carted it round, begging for a penny for the guy, and then it was going to be put on the bonfire. But it hadn't been, at least not the same one. Did they get scared at the last moment and chuck it in the stream? Perhaps they'd always intended to do it that way. The bonfire would keep its secret for the time being — it'd be days before it was cold and dead. As cold and dead as the midget.

But who'd do a thing like that? Tig thought he had a good idea about that. The red and white scarf which had been wrapped round the guy's head, that was the thing to go for.

About half an hour before the end of afternoon school he put up his hand and was given permission to leave the room. He slipped along the corridor, out through the back door, across the playground, hoping nobody would notice him, and made the safety of the hedge at the side of the playing-field. Getting from there to the common and the path to the town was easy. There was a man walking his dog near the bonfire, but that was all. An iron box would be safe enough there for a bit of time yet. Tig went on. He knew where he was going.

There were several junior schools scattered about the town. Tig had known one of them very well, but the one whose colours were red and white was less familiar. He had recognised the colours, of course, and he knew where the school was. It meant crossing the centre of the town, and he had to be careful there. It might amuse *him* to give the police the slip, but he could hardly expect them to join in the joke.

He passed right under the windows of the police station — it seemed safer than to cross the road and use the opposite pavement. Any policeman who was looking out would hardly notice what was going on right under his nose. There were plenty of people about, and that made it easier to slip through. There were advantages, after all, in being small.

He was stopped once by an acquaintance of his mother's who wanted, she said, to say how sorry she was, but who in reality merely wished to extract information. Tig glared and mumbled, thereby increasing his reputation for being difficult. When he saw someone else whom his mother knew he ran across the street.

He was annoyed with himself for doing it — not because it was impolite (that didn't worry him at all), but because his embarrassment was something he wanted to hide. What had happened was nothing to do with anybody else. He brushed his feelings away with a quick sprint down the road, and concentrated on the job in hand.

He found the school he was looking for, in a back-street, away from the shops and heavy traffic. There were little groups of women waiting and gossiping round the entrance. It was an elderly red-brick building, with stone-mullioned windows set high in the walls, and steep gables. A tower, looking as though it had strayed from some ancient castle, sprouted from the roof and covered a black and rusty bell. Further down the road, there was a little tobacco and newspaper shop on the corner. Tig became absorbed in the contents of the window. He could keep a good watch from there — the plate-glass acted as a sort of mirror.

It was not long before children began to stream out from the big main door in the middle of the building. Tig breathed a little sigh of relief: things were working out the way he'd hoped. There was quite a lot of red and white in evidence. It was a chilly day and many of the children had the familiar scarves. Tig concentrated on the plate-glass window.

Some children ran to their mothers and were bundled off to their tea; others stood about in small groups, either waiting, or perhaps filling in time because they had nothing better to do. There was a game of 'he' going on round the prams, and even a conker or two. It all, Tig thought, looked very young.

The owner of the shop came out and stared at him. Tig stared back.

"Want anything, son?" He was a big burly man, not one to be ignored. Tig moved a few yards, and stood with his hands in his pockets slouching against the wall.

There was one little party of children running off down the road, playing football with an empty tin which rattled against the kerb-stones. Three or four of them there seemed to be. One was a girl with long bright red hair which flew behind her like the tail of a comet.

One foot on the pavement and the other in the gutter, Tig lazily fell in behind.

Seventeen

TIG was fast learning the business of trailing. Having lived all his fourteen years on the edge of a town, he had acquired a certain basic knowledge of both town and country. He had known two playgrounds, the street and the woodland. The first had taught him to deal with people, the second with himself.

On this occasion he was reasonably sure that the little group of kids ahead of him, pushing, shoving, shouting, was unaware of his presence. People passed along the street, and he was just one of them, a boy with a thin face and short spiky hair, dirty blue jeans, and an elderly anorak. Nothing special.

The group crossed the town. Tig found himself once more on the edge of the common. He was afraid to follow them there because it would look obvious, but he made a guess which point they were making for, and raced round the edge, keeping a wary eye open, using the cover of the hedges, fences, and streets.

There was a bench with an old man sitting on it reading a newspaper. Tig sat down with him so that he could watch the common's edge and at the same time shelter behind the old man's paper. After a moment or two, the old man who thought Tig had been trying to read the sports page on the back of the paper, offered it to him with the comment: "Here, you can have it. Nothing but trouble in it." Tig gratefully accepted the paper. The old man crossed his hands over his waistcoat and closed his eyes, but after a few minutes he came to with a start, said, "It's getting dark. Time for me tea," and wandered off into the twilight. Tig spread the paper wide.

He had not long to wait. The group of children, with the girl at the head, burst through the bushes and spilled into the road a hundred yards away. Tig watched to see which way they went.

They seemed to be making for an area of neglected woodland. On this side the town faded into ramshackle decay rather than came to any definite end. There were farms further on, but here a belt of wild forgotten woods had escaped the bulldozer and the axe. The trees showed black and solemn against the pale blue of the evening sky. There was no fog tonight. Stars were beginning to appear. It felt almost like the beginning of a frost. Tig shivered.

The children had disappeared inside the wood. Tig stayed behind a bush, wondering whether to follow them in. There was a chance they had some further objective in view, but that was a chance he had to take. If he went in after them, all the advantages were on their side. They knew the place, he didn't. It was getting dark, and any moment a careless step would reveal his presence. He waited. It was getting cold.

He thought he could see a light flickering among the trees, a brief spark, repeated irregularly, as though someone was sending a message. For a moment Tig considered the idea. He tried to drag back into his mind what he had once taught himself of the morse code, but he came to the conclusion that the flashes of light were too disconnected for that.

Then the flashes coalesced into a dull red glow, and he smelled smoke. What on earth had they got there, these kids who looked so little but who seemed to have so much freedom? The youngest had appeared to be about nine, the eldest no more than eleven. Besides the red-haired girl there had been two boys and another of indeterminate sex. Tig thought back into the deep past, and tried to remember the sort of things he'd done when he was that age. It was a long time ago.

So they had some sort of camp-fire going. And who could blame them? Tig said to himself. A very sensible bunch of kids. At least it made one thing certain: they weren't going anywhere else. Tig went on waiting and watching, crouched in a shallow ditch behind the hedge.

He was puzzled by the loneliness of the place. It wasn't far from the town, ten minutes' walk perhaps, but he hadn't seen a soul come along this lane. No houses. No sign of life. Not even a car. Perhaps the lane didn't lead anywhere? Tig tried to think just where he was on the map. He ought to know, he told himself, but his wanderings in the past had never, so far as he remembered, brought him to this hidden valley with its dark and secret wood.

He was so engrossed with his thoughts that the children had reappeared on the road before he noticed them. He froze into immobility. The children were silent, unnaturally so, Tig thought. They walked quietly and demurely along the lane, four little figures, dark-outlined and defenceless. The girl's red hair blazed in the last light of day.

Tig heard her say one sentence, though he caught only a few words of it, but he recognised the voice, a high, whining voice. He had heard it before, when the monstrous idea of the pram and the Guy Fawkes came into his mind. It was an unmistakable voice. She said something about tea-time, and then broke into a helter-skelter run, pursued by the other three. Their feet clattered on the stones, and then there was silence.

Tig rose.

He had learned very little so far. Having come this far, it was silly not to go on. There was no one about as he crossed the road and entered the darkness of the wood. He could still see the red glow ahead, and he used this to guide him.

The path was narrow and low, even for him, little more than a tunnel through the undergrowth. The trees had lofty trunks stretching to the light and protecting all sorts of smaller vegetation at their roots. Tig noticed that the path beneath his feet was clear of obstruction and remarkably dry. He had expected mud.

A clearing opened out abruptly. It was no more than twenty yards square, secret and enclosed. A dell, perhaps a natural one, perhaps the result of random clay digging in some past age, had been gradually surrounded by trees and bushes, cut off by nature from the comparative civilisation round it. In the middle of the dell, which was perhaps five feet lower than the rest of the wood, a hut had been built. It looked old. It must have been first put together many years before it had been discovered by its present occupants. It looked like the work of a tramp, some permanent home for a wanderer to come back to, sure that it would not have been disturbed. It had a good solid framework of four posts, sides of planks, a sloping roof covered with turf, one little window filled with a sheet of opaque plastic, and a good solid door which had clearly been removed from some greatly superior building. Cracks round its sides were plugged with newspaper.

In front of the door, and a few feet away, was the fire, damped down with leaves which produced a thick column of smoke rising straight into the motionless air. The whole place had an atmosphere that was almost cosy.

Tig looked about him with astonishment. Strange that this little hidden world should exist so near the town. He wondered whether anyone else knew about it besides himself and the kids' gang with their red-haired boss. Unlikely. If anyone else got to know, it wouldn't last five minutes. They'd interfere, and say it wasn't nice. A health hazard, or something like that.

How long had he got? He wanted a good look round, that was for sure, but he didn't want to get caught. He'd have to work fast, but not so fast that he disturbed things and made his presence obvious. Fallen leaves covered the ground — that was good. They wouldn't show any clear footprints.

Tig stepped carefully round the fire to the door of the hut. He pushed it experimentally, and was surprised when it opened without any hindrance. Not a squeak. Careless of them. The door had a perfectly good lock. Perhaps they'd lost the key.

Tig peered into the blackness. There was so little light left in the sky now that he could make out only a square box in the middle and a pile of old newspapers against the wall. He decided to risk it.

He tore a sheet off one of the newspapers, folded it quickly into a spill, and lit it at the red-glowing fire. That was better. The flickering light revealed little that he had not already seen: a few grubby mugs on the table, a blackened frying-pan, a lidless kettle, a box of matches, four dusty orange-boxes. The light burned down to his fingers, and he pushed the remains of the paper into the ashes of the fire. He closed the door.

Tig needed to think. He sat by the fire hugging his knees and staring into the wavering glow. He had worked out in his own mind what he thought had happened — the newspaper-seller, the alley, the pram, and the Guy Fawkes. But there was the same difficulty as with the problem about the musicians — how do you prove it, so that someone else will believe it? Could these little kids have really done what he believed they had? If they had killed the little bloke, wouldn't they have just run off and pretended they were miles away? But they *had* run away. When Tig went down the alley by the White Lion, there had been nobody there — he was sure of that — certainly not these kids. But somebody had moved the body afterwards. It wasn't there when the copper went to look. How long after was that? An hour, or a half-hour? Long enough to come back. But why come back? Tig thought he could understand that. They'd knocked him down and taken his money, and they'd be standing there while the little guy lay at their feet, without moving. And they'd be scared, and run. But then they'd wonder — was he really dead? Only one way to find out — they'd have to come back to see, hoping perhaps that he'd have got up and walked away. But he hadn't got up. The blood would have spread a bit further. What could they do? They must take it away so that no one would find it. Bundle it into the pram, put a scarf round its head to hide those staring eyes, and the blood. Wheel it round the town, have people say, "What a good guy!" collect the money. But not for ever. They'd have to do something. Into the bonfire? That would be the best idea. But would it all burn? If it didn't, it would be found, people would know. Another guy would have to do. Wheel the pram away. Tip it up by the stream. Perhaps it would be washed away to sea. That would be the end of it.

Tig went on staring into the fire. He'd have to do something about the bonfire on the common sooner or later. But that could wait. It wouldn't walk away.

Tig sighed. His legs were stiff, and he got up to stretch. Something large and angular behind the hut caught his eye as he looked round. He went to investigate.

The pram.

If only there was a bit more light. The moon had risen now, but it was nowhere near full. The little dell looked as though it were covered with a silver wash, taking away all colour and leaving only a shiny deceptive sketch, full of meaningless shadows.

He stared into the fire for some time after that. He knew that they must come back, else why would they have lit the fire? He was waiting for them. He listened to the little noises of the trees, the occasional movement of a piece of wood on the fire, the eerie whining of the air through the branches.

The footsteps, when they came, were quiet, muffled by the fallen leaves.

Tig stood up and moved without a sound to the edge of the circle. He had marked out one tree some time before, a solid trunk, a branch near the ground. One foot on the branch, a hand-hold, a swing, another foot. Repeat. Easy.

His body was braced against the trunk, held by encircling branches. He was above them, and he could see. That was all that mattered.

Four little figures entered the clearing. They were busy and purposeful. They all had something to do. Some sort of practised ritual of domesticity was being carried out, and in a minute, the fire was bright, and four boxes stood in a square round it. The kettle swung on a pole over the flames, the mugs were placed ready, and a spoonful of some brown powder was placed in the bottom of each. There was a certain amount of chatter, but nothing irrelevant to the business in hand. A religious efficiency ordered all their movement and speech. Four little figures sat on four boxes, gazing into the fire.

Then the chanting began, slow and quiet at first, gradually increasing, but never reaching a height. The tune sounded like a variation of 'London's burning'. The words were difficult to hear, but as the sound grew louder, it became possible to make them out.

"Boil the kettle, boil the kettle,
See it boil, see it boil:
Steam! Steam!
Pour the water, pour the water."

It was an innocent sound, a childish chant. Tig felt embarrassed to listen to it. Had he been wrong?

The girl with red hair organised the making of whatever it was they had in their mugs. Steam rose and mingled with the column of smoke. Four little figures sat with their fingers curled round their mugs, but they did not drink. They seemed to be waiting for some sort of signal, the nature of which escaped Tig's eyes.

The four mugs were put carefully on the ground, the four figures stood, raised their arms to shoulder-height, joined hands. It was all like some ancient religious rite which had to be performed exactly if the gods were to be pleased.

There was five seconds' silence, and then, with a heart-stopping suddenness, they howled. Just one short stab of barbaric high-pitched noise, and they sat down again, satisfied and unconcerned.

The girl with red hair looked straight at the tree where Tig was concealed.

"You can come down," she said.

Eighteen

TIG felt very foolish. The one overwhelming question: how had she known?, could be answered in only one way. He slithered to the ground, careless now of the noise he made and the twigs he snapped, and strolled easily towards the group by the fire. His eyes were wary. He knew that his every movement was being watched, and that as a stranger he was an enemy. He kept his hands in his pockets.

"Well?" he said, lightly.

All four kept their gaze fixed on him, but said nothing.

"What you doing here?" the girl demanded at length. She sounded annoyed rather than frightened.

"It's a free country," Tig said. "This your camp, then?"

The girl ignored the question.

"How did you get here?"

"Me own two feet. What's it to you?"

"Anyone with you?"

"No."

"What do you want?"

"Just to say hello."

"You're a *spy*!" The words shot out, sharp and venomous.

The other three got up slowly and moved in a circle round him. Tig stood still, his hands still deep in his pockets. The three began to dance round him, shouting,

"Spy! Spy! *Spy!*" Tig grinned again. Just *kids*. Playing. He pushed through the circle and sat on a box by the fire opposite the girl with red hair. The other three, their circle broken, stood around forlornly, as though some convention had been violated and they didn't know how to deal with it.

"Oh, cut it out!" Tig said. "Tell 'em to sit down and shut up."

The girl made a quick movement with her hand, and the three dropped to the ground, their eyes bright in the glow of the fire.

"That's better. I want to talk to you. What's your name?"

"My name's my own," the girl said.

"Have it your own way. It's just you four, OK?"

The girl nodded briefly.

"What do you call yourselves? Some fancy name, I bet."

One of the boys shifted, and said solemnly: "We're the Baddens. She's our captain." His confidence brought him a quick kick from his captain, and he subsided.

"The Baddens, eh? That fits."

The girl looked at him contemptuously.

"Nice little secret place you've got, anyway," Tig said admiringly. Better jolly her along for a bit, he thought, then make her angry, and she might say something useful.

"How did you know I was here?"

The girl shrugged. "I'm not blind."

"Well, I thought I was pretty well hidden. You didn't look as though you knew."

"I knew."

"How?"

"There's a piece of paper jammed in the door at the top. We always leave it like that when we go. Then if it isn't there when we come back, we know somebody's been."

"That's good," Tig said. "Clever!" And in fact he *was* impressed: he hadn't noticed that piece of paper.

"So you knew somebody had been. But I might have gone away."

"Your face shows up. It didn't take long to spot you."

"That *is* good," Tig said. "So you come here and make coffee. Or tea? Got a spare cup?"

"No."

"Up to you. What else do you do?"

"You'd better go." The girl stood up, and as she did so, the other three scrambled to their feet.

Tig made no movement. "I'm not going."

"We'll make you."

"You, and who else?"

"Spy!"

"*Spy! Spy! Spy!*"

Tig made himself more comfortable on the box.

"Now look," he said. "I just happened to drop in, see? Calm down. I'm not going to hurt you."

"You couldn't." The girl's voice was contemptuous.

"Want to try?"

"There's four of us. And we've got help."

"Where's the help? Up the trees?"

"You wouldn't understand."

"I could get out of here whenever I want," Tig said. "So sit down. I'm staying for a bit, and I'll go when I decide. Right?"

The girl stared at him with hot angry eyes. Her hair shone like flame in the light of the fire. Then abruptly she sat.

"The Badden will get you," she said, gazing into the fire.

Tig watched her. What the hell was she talking about? The Badden? It sounded like some weird devil or hobgoblin out of a book. She didn't believe that bunk, surely?

"Prove it," he said, sneering.

Her head jerked up. Her eyes stared into his. They were no longer angry, but cold and calculating.

"Have you got any money?" she demanded.

Tig was surprised. "Why?"

"It needs money."

"Well, it'll have to wait. Not a penny."

"True?"

"True as I'm sitting here."

"It needs money," she repeated.

"What does? Your precious devil?"

"How do you know?" The words were quiet and menacing. There was no movement from any of the four.

"How do you know about the Badden? Have you seen? Are you one of his?"

"One of his what?" Tig said, uncertainly.

The girl went on staring at him. At length she sighed and said, "We'll have to find out. The Test."

There was a little stir among the other three. Tig sat still.

"The Test," the girl said again. "We'll have to have the Test."

A sombre complete silence fell on the dell in the middle of the wood. The slight breeze had dropped, the branches of the trees stood motionless, the moon shone clear. Not even a distant car to break the soundlessness. The rest of the world where other people lived and died seemed a very long way off.

Tig wondered whether to get up and walk away. Half of what these strange little kids said was incomprehensible. Certainly, he had heard nothing so far to confirm or refute his ideas about the pram. And what was this Test? Something that impressed the others, evidently. Their eyes stared at him with manifest wonder. Not that he was afraid, Tig said to himself. It sounded as though he were trying to convince himself against his better judgement. With surprise he realised that he was, as it were, standing outside himself, watching his own reactions, and laughing at them. Well, he *wasn't* afraid, anyway. If it came to a punch-up, he ought to be a match for them, all of them together.

Tig decided to wait and see what happened. He tried to create the impression that he didn't care, but his muscles were tense and ready.

The girl with red hair went to the hut and came back

with a wooden spoon. Nothing special, Tig noticed, just the sort of thing you'd find in a kitchen.

The girl pointed the spoon solemnly at each of the other three in turn. Gravely each one touched the spoon and nodded his head.

"The Test shall be done," she announced. "We are all agreed."

"Sounds like school," Tig said. "Exams and things. What do I do? Recite tables?"

The girl paid no attention. The four moved away from the fire, leaving Tig on his box. With the spoon she marked out a rough square in the fallen leaves round the fire, including Tig, but not the others.

"Magic?" Tig enquired.

"Yes," said the girl without emotion. "It always works."

"What does it do? Keep the wild rabbits away?"

The girl ignored the sneer. She marked three places opposite Tig, and the smaller ones sat there in a line. The heat and the smoke from the fire made it difficult to see them properly, but their eyes flickered in the light. They seemed to be holding out their hands, palm upwards, towards the fire, as though begging.

"You've rehearsed it well, I'll give you that," Tig said. Though he wouldn't have admitted it, he was glad the fire was between him and those three little images the other side. Like so many undersized devils, sitting there gloating. They'd started their silly chanting again, as well.

"Boil the kettle, boil the kettle,
See it boil, see it boil:
Steam! Steam!
Pour the water, pour the water."

Low and threatening was the song, repeated again and again, each time a little louder than the time before.

"Polly put the kettle on, we'll all have tea," Tig said. "Pass the sugar." He said it lightly, but he wished that mournful chanting would stop. And what was that devilish girl up to now?

Her red hair was loose about her shoulders like a blood-red cloak. She held the wooden spoon before her, turning it slowly round and round in her hand. And all the time the chanting grew and the fierce little eyes stared at him through the smoke.

"Aw, come on!" said Tig. "You can do better than this. I want to see a bit of real conjuring, if it isn't way past your bed-time." He was still hoping to make the girl angry, but she remained unruffled by his words. "Why don't you turn yourself into a frog and hop off?"

With a sudden movement the girl plunged the wooden spoon into the lidless kettle which hung over the fire, and stirred the hot water.

" 'Bout time for a drink," Tig commented. "What have you got? Coffee with a dash of rum?"

Still the girl took no notice of him. Her lips moved in time with the chanting from the other three, but no sound except a whispered hiss came from her lips, matching the hissing from the kettle. She lifted the spoon and held it upright in her two hands as high as she could.

"Boil the kettle, boil the kettle,
See it boil, see it boil:
Steam! Steam!
Pour the water, pour the water."

The chant grew to a shout, and then stopped completely.

"That's better," said Tig. "It was getting on my nerves."

The girl slowly lowered the spoon and looked at the kettle. Steam was rising from the bubbling surface of the water.

"The water is ready," she said.

"I can see that. Where's the mugs then?"

"You don't need a mug."

"Thanks very much," Tig said.

"The Test," the girl announced. She sounded almost as

though she had lost interest in her strange ritual, but the eyes of the others still stared at Tig, unwavering.

"So you said."

"You put the thumb of your left hand in the water."

Tig was startled. He didn't know what he had expected, but it certainly wasn't this.

"You must be joking!"

"The thumb. Your left hand. That is the Test. We've all done it. Look!" The girl extended her left hand in front of Tig's face. There was a noticeable scar, and the nail looked as though it had been hit with a hammer.

"All right, all right." Tig peered into the depths of the kettle. There was only about an inch of water in it, but it wasn't a nice prospect. Tig wondered whether it might be possible to curl his hand round inside the kettle, without touching the water at all. There was still the steam, though. Was it worth it? It seemed the way to gain the confidence of these odd creatures, and he might learn something from them. He remembered the face of the little guy in the alley with the blood all over his face.

"How long?" he said.

"While we say the song."

"The water boiling one?"

"The song."

"OK, the song, then. You like your bit of play-acting, don't you?" Tig looked round at the staring eyes. They watched him with monstrous fascination.

"Nice friendly lot you are, aren't you? The sort that'd beat a cat to death just for the kicks."

"Not cats."

Tig glanced quickly at her. "People?"

"It needs money," she said calmly. "Money is precious. It works with money."

"What does?"

The girl shook herself impatiently.

"Are you afraid? Scared?"

"No, I'm not," Tig said stoutly. He put out his hand

towards the kettle. The steam curled about his fingers, hot and stinging. Now or never.

He made a fist of his hand, as tight as he could, and began to lower it through the steam. Four pairs of eyes stared gloatingly at his every movement. Mouths opened, and the low chant began.

"Boil, the kettle, boil the kettle . . ."

Tig's eyes were fixed on his left hand. He was trying desperately to keep it still in the scalding steam. Would their silly chant never end? He did not see the girl raise the wooden spoon. With a vicious smack she brought it down on Tig's wrist.

Nineteen

TIG'S hand was in the boiling water for only a second, but it was enough. He was so astounded that he was unable to make any sound, though he opened his mouth for the scream which never came. He hugged the damaged hand to his chest. He looked at his clenched fist, and then at the girl, with an unbelieving horror.

"Doesn't hurt for long," the girl said, in a matter-of-fact voice. She was still swinging the wooden spoon up and down. "You passed. If you'd shouted, you wouldn't have." Tig tried to think of something to say which didn't sound silly. There was nothing. He pulled out a handkerchief to wrap round his fingers, but the girl said. "Better to leave it open to the air. Won't hurt so much."

"How do you know?" Tig growled, then realised that this question as well was silly. He stood up, his left hand held away from his side to prevent it rubbing against his clothes.

"Finished?"

"There's a bit more."

Tig clenched his fists again. He was going to be prepared this time.

"You have to go to the Badden."

"What Badden?"

"You'll see."

"But what if I say I'm not going?"

"You have to." The girl sounded surprised. "Don't you want to?"

"No," said Tig, and he meant it. "I'm off."

"You can't go," the girl insisted. "You have to finish the Test. Now that you've started, you can't refuse." Her eyes glittered in the firelight, and Tig found himself drawn by curiosity. His hand was hurting less now. He didn't think it was badly burned — the skin seemed all right as he tentatively examined it. Might peel perhaps, like sunburn, and leave a scar to add to the others which covered his hands. He'd be more careful this time, though.

"OK," he said.

"You're coming?"

"That's what I said."

She led her party through the clearing to the circle of trees.

"It'll be dark. We know the way. Take my hand."

Despite a primitive embarrassment, Tig saw the reason for doing so. He scrambled up the slope from the dell to the level ground, and walked with his guide through the thick network of tree trunks and undergrowth. It seemed, Tig thought as he held his left hand away from him, that this wood had more than its fair share of holly and bramble. He wondered what he was being led to, and a number of possibilities, some frightening, some merely ludicrous, flashed through his mind. An elephant trap, with pointed stakes fixed in the bottom? A stream for total immersion? Or the thud of a piece of timber on his head, followed by a black insensibility? He knew just one thing about this girl — that he didn't trust her an inch. Not after the wooden spoon.

What sort of path it was beneath his feet he couldn't see. He was aware of old dry leaves and the smell of earth. The trees covered the path, and the moon could pierce the tracery of branches only intermittently. Once he was told to keep his head down. He was walking in some sort of tunnel, the top of which would have come up to his chest if he had gone upright. Deer, he knew, made this sort of track, and there were deer in the countryside around, though he had seen them only once.

And then they came to another clearing, smaller than the camp-site, more covert and secluded. There was a gap in the tree-cover, through which the white light of the moon poured down with a brilliance that seemed intolerable after the close darkness of the tunnel. It was very quiet. The girl and the three others stood in a solemn row at the edge. They had pushed Tig to the front, and he stumbled on a tree-root and fell to one knee. His injured hand scraped against the earth.

"Look!" said the girl, in a whisper. "Look straight ahead."

"What at?" Tig demanded. He raised his head to gaze round, but all he could see was the dark skirting of trees, and the colourless deep hole of the sky.

"Look!" said the girl again.

Tig became aware of an awkward and angular shape among the trees opposite, something that seemed to stick out from the straight lines of the branches. Two small points of light gleamed dimly.

For the first time Tig knew real fear. He wanted to run, to scream — anything to break the horrible stillness of those awful children standing in a stiff line behind him, anything to cover up those two eyes of malevolent light.

Was there something alive there? Some wild animal, or one half-tamed by its four worshippers? Or was it just a trick of the moonlight and the shadows?

The twin points of light glared unwinking. There was no sound, not even of his own breathing. Slowly, Tig got to his feet. He stood in the same stiff attitude as the other four. He forced himself to breathe, and as he expelled the air he had bottled up in his lungs, and took in great gasps of clean fresh air, reason returned. He moved a step or two towards the strange dark shape among the trees.

Something large barred his way, with great spikes

stretching up from its head.

He put out a hand and felt fur. But it was cold and dead, no suggestion of living warmth. No movement.

An enormous stag, its antlers branching in pride, its legs stiff, standing on a wooden base.

Stuffed.

Glass eyes twinkling.

The hair on its nose beginning to fall out.

A poor old stuffed stag.

Tig turned and laughed.

"Where did you get old Harry from?"

Rage flickered in the girl's eyes. She ran towards him and beat her fists on his chest.

"Hey! Watch it!" Tig said, calmly. He grabbed her wrists, trying to keep her hands away. She was a strong little creature.

"Don't want to hurt your feelings," he said, "but it's good for a laugh."

She twisted away and kicked him viciously in the shins. Tig cursed. "What did you do that for?" He rubbed his leg with his uninjured hand. She attacked him again, and Tig found himself flat on his chest, his mouth full of leaves. He raised his head. The two fore-legs of the stag rose in front of his face like shaggy sticks. The left one had been eaten away at the hoof, leaving a gap between it and the black wooden base.

Tig pulled himself round and sat on the base, his head just below the stag's. He felt safer there, protected by the great furry body at his back.

"You keep away!" he told the girl. She stood in front of him, clenching and unclenching her fists. The other three had not moved from their place at the opposite side of the clearing.

Tig looked down at his left hand. He understood now about the kettle and the boiling water. You had to become like the stag with the injured leg to be one of his. One of the Badden's.

"Where did you find it?" he asked. "The furry friend."

"He came, that's all." The girl was still angry, but for the moment Tig realised she could do nothing. What had she expected to happen when he sat up here with the stag for company? The sky to fall in? Well, it hadn't.

"Aw, come off it!" he said. "That's good enough for the tiddlers. You know better than that."

The girl shook her red hair. "He came. He needs money."

"Who doesn't?" Tig said lightly. "What does he do with it?"

"He gives it back to us." The girl's words were reluctant, but forced out of her because of Tig's seat of protection at the feet of the stag. Tig wondered how much of this rubbish she believed.

"I see," he said. "Just like a bank. Handy. Where does he get it from?"

The girl's eyes dropped. Her red hair sprawled over her shoulders.

"Come on! You tell me. Where do you get it from? The money."

The girl was silent.

Tig lazily extricated himself from the grasp of the stag. He advanced towards her. He knew he had got her scared, and he intended to press home his advantage. Her hold over the other three clearly depended on their faith in the power of the stag, a faith which she did not want broken. Again Tig wondered how much she herself believed. And where on earth had she got this stuffed animal from? He remembered seeing stags' heads in pictures of castles and big houses. Perhaps this had come from some big house that got knocked down or destroyed by vandals. It made a good trophy . . .

Deliberately he turned his back on her. He stretched up a hand and snatched at a leather purse which hung from one of the antlers.

"This is where the money comes from, is it?" He turned

slowly to face the girl and found all four of them right on his heels. "You steal, do you? And you hang up your silly little trophies on his poor old antlers, do you? How many have you got, then?"

He whirled about and filled his hands with the purses and bags which hung on the antlers like apples on a tree.

"A nice bit of common thievery, eh? And a bit of play-acting to dress it up? You've got them to believe it all? Well, where's the money?"

The girl spun round to face the other three.

"Don't listen!" she commanded. "He's a spy! The Badden will get him. You'll see!" There was a note of hysteria in her voice.

"You listen to me!" Tig roared. "She's got you to do the thieving, hasn't she? And all the money came here, didn't it? And here are the bags and the wallets and purses. Well, go on, ask her. Where's the money?"

The three smaller ones still stood in a solemn line, their hands stiffly at their sides, their faces white and impassive.

"Where's the money?" Tig roared again. "Go on, ask her! What's she done with it? You never saw any of it, did you? Here! Just look at these bags. Take this one!"

He held out a large black wallet with a long strap.

"Go, on, take it! It had money in it once."

The other three made no movement. The girl stared at them as though willing them to hold to their belief.

Tig stared too, but at the black leather pouch in his hand. The moonlight shone palely on the lettering printed on its side, worn and dirty, but still decipherable.

"So you *did* do it! You killed him! It's the wallet the midget who sold papers used, isn't it? Look what it says along the side. Go on! Look, damn you!"

The girl stayed motionless, but her eyes blazed with sudden panic.

"It's a lie! We didn't! All we did was knock him down. Honest!" Her voice rose to a whine.

Tig let his arm fall to his side.

"OK," he said flatly. "You win."

What did it matter any more? He was tired. He wanted to get away. There was a dull throbbing in his left hand which was repeated in his brain. Who cared?

"How do I get out?" he said. It was a surrender.

The girl seemed to grow as Tig slouched. He could understand the power she had over the rest of the group. She knew she had won. Her eyes glittered with triumph.

"Follow me," she ordered, and like a little boy who had lost his way Tig took her hand and allowed himself to be led. They came to the dell where the hut stood black in the moonlight. The fire's embers glowed dully.

"You know the way from here," she said.

"OK."

As he stumbled along the path to the road he could hear them kicking the fire together. What was the time? It seemed late, and he was bone-tired, but when he glanced at his watch, he saw it was only half-past seven. He wanted to curl up somewhere quiet and close his eyes.

But his head was too full of thoughts to allow him any rest.

So all they had done was knock him down. That's what she'd said. Honest. Who *had* killed him then? He'd be lying there in the gutter, moaning a bit perhaps. Hurt. But not so hurt that he couldn't see what was going on at the back of the White Lion Hotel. They'd seen him there, those two with the flute and the violin. They'd seen Tig, too, but he'd got away. What would they do? They'd think about it a bit, come back, find the poor little old bloke still lying there, and finish him off.

What was it he'd heard one of them say later in the hut where they lived? They'd been talking about, Tig, and the man with the black beard had said, "One more wouldn't have made much difference." One *more*.

Tig tramped on into the town.

Twenty

INSPECTOR Roberts was working late that evening. "Any ideas?" he asked Sergeant Steadman.

Steadman placidly stroked his chin.

"Well, sir, what have we got? Two villains charged with multiple robbery. Seven cases all within three miles of the town, and all inside the last two months. No suspicion of their activities up to now. Well-known as street musicians round the place — and very good ones as well, I'm told, sir, high-brow stuff at that. It makes a good cover for them, especially when the younger one dresses up as quite a passable woman. Sharp of that boy to have noticed it."

"Yes," Roberts interrupted. "And where is that damned boy?"

"He'll be found, sir."

"We need him, Jack, badly. The other case. The newspaper-seller."

"Quite so, sir. But we're doing pretty well with the robberies, there's that to consider. The amount of stuff we found in that shed this morning is worth a fair bit."

"H'm," Roberts growled. "They had a nice set-up, Jack. Where so many villains go wrong is to try to get rid of the stuff too soon. The word gets around, the narks start squealing, and there's a lead to work on. But these didn't. They had it all stashed away there. I think their idea was to run this town for a bit, then move on to some other place.

Being a street musician means you can stand around and watch buildings without causing comment. We're still missing a bit, though."

"The coin collection, sir?"

"Just that. It's odd about those coins. If we had them, we could tie in those two with the White Lion job, and probably the paper-seller as well. But they're not saying a word, damn them."

"There's another thing, sir."

"H'm?"

"The accomplice, sir, inside the hotel."

Roberts groaned. "Confound it," he muttered. "But the boy said he saw someone at the window passing a case out to the two in the alley. It all comes back to that boy, Jack. Where the devil is he?"

It was shortly after this that Tig, footsore and weary, turned up at the police station. He didn't particularly want to come, because he remembered his previous efforts to convince authority that he was not playing jokes. But when he trudged up the steps and stood at the counter, a vision of sausage and eggs and baked beans came into his mind so forcibly that he thought he could almost smell it. His reception was gratifying. He was whisked upstairs to Inspector Roberts's office with so much despatch that you might have thought they were scared of losing him. Tig grinned quietly to himself. He had a nice comfortable chair, and if he played his cards right . . .

"Ready for a cup of tea, lad?" Steadman enquired.

Tig nodded.

"Hungry?"

Tig nodded again. He pushed his hands on the arms of the chair, all ready to go. Roberts interrupted.

"There's a few questions first."

Tig sighed. He might have known. Nothing in this world was free. He was still clutching the flat leather pouch he had removed from the stag's antlers, and he now placed it face-downwards on the desk. Roberts took no notice of it.

"The man at the window," Roberts began. "A description, that's what we want."

"Couldn't see properly," Tig said. He had a literal mind. They hadn't asked him if he knew who it was, so there was no reason to tell them, yet. He hugged this little piece of information to himself with pleasure. They ought to be able to work it out. That's what they were paid for.

"Tall? Short? Thin? What sort of hair? Glasses?"

Tig shifted irritably. It didn't matter, that could wait. He turned over the flat leather pouch so that the lettering was visible.

"*Evening Herald?*" Roberts read. His eyes narrowed with suspicion. "The newspaper-seller's bag. What do you know about that?"

That's right, Tig said to himself, blame it on me. He forced himself to be reasonable and coherent. He told them of the gang of children, the hut in the wood, the stuffed stag, and the trophies hanging from its antlers.

Then he had to tell them all over again. Tig's voice fell on the silence of the room in a dull monotone. Two pairs of eyes watched him shrewdly, and two minds wondered if they could believe a word of it.

They let him go eventually, and the same motherly woman P.C. took him down to the canteen and fed him with sausages and chips and baked beans.

"Getting to be quite a habit," she remarked.

Tig made no reply: he was busy.

Upstairs in the office Steadman was reading aloud the notes he had been making of Tig's story. In his dry uninflected voice, it seemed even less probable. When he had finished, he laid the note-book on his knee, and looked at Roberts. Roberts ran a pencil through his grey hair.

"Any truth in it, Jack?"

"What he's said has proved right so far, sir."

"Apart from a false name and address."

"Understandable, sir, in the circumstances. Trouble at school."

"H'm. So you think it rings true. Frankly, I don't. A gang of kids, I ask you! Ages between nine and eleven. They're only babies. Children don't behave like that."

"Don't they, sir? I can remember going around with a gang at that age. Some pretty odd things we got up to."

"More revelations from a copper's past?" Roberts enquired sarcastically.

Steadman looked at the grey hole of the window, lit by an orange glow of street lamps outside.

"It's a funny thing, sir. I've noticed it with my own kids. The difference between fact and fantasy, sir; it's an indistinct line. I've seen it said that the comics have a lot to do with it, and cartoons, and that sort of thing. You see a man batter another on the head with a brick, and the next picture is full of stars — wham! — and after that he's OK. No ill effects whatever. So you translate that into real life, thinking that the same results will follow, but life is a bit different from the comics."

"But this girl with the red hair that young English talks about. Think she's real? Snatching bags at her age? Whatever next!" Roberts sounded scandalised.

"It happens, sir, as you well know." Steadman became reflective again. "I call to mind, sir, something that occurred when I was about nine."

Roberts groaned, but Steadman ploughed on.

"There were half a dozen of us, I suppose. I still see one or two of them. Charlie Hunt was a wrong 'un, but it didn't amount to much then. The odd packet of sweets when the shop-keeper wasn't looking, that sort of thing. We had a hide-out at the back of a derelict house, all gone now, of course, and we used to meet there and swap jokes and share a packet of Woodbines. You remember those packets of five? Well, one day someone else came barging in by accident. I can still remember his face, white and pimpled, just covered with spots. We caught him and grilled him a bit, but he wasn't saying anything. So we tied him to the banisters at the bottom of the stairs with a bit of old rope.

And then we cleared off." Steadman stopped for a moment, and Roberts watched him silently.

"We didn't mean any real harm, of course. Just to teach him a lesson not to come snooping into our territory. But we forgot about him. We forgot about him until late that night. He'd been there all day, tied to the banisters, and he'd struggled with the ropes till his hands were bleeding and he'd nearly strangled himself. He'd torn part of the banisters away, and they'd come down on top of him and knocked him out. We thought he was dead. Made quite an impression on me, that did, sir. Of course, he came round, and we took him home, and it turned out all right. But it was some time before the gang met again. We were all about the same age. About nine or ten. Kids don't change much. All familiar stuff, of course. Usual argument."

Steadman's calm voice came to a stop, and there was silence. Roberts shifted in his chair.

"A kids' prank," he said. "You must have money nowadays, and it doesn't matter how you get it. All that money laid out on the window of the paper-seller's hut. A dark night. A knock on the head. Just a bit of adventure. He should have got up and walked away, but he didn't."

Roberts sighed heavily. "We'll have to check. Get that boy up again. We shall need a few more facts. He might be more helpful now he's been fed."

When Tig appeared in Roberts's office again, the tiredness had dropped from him. Steadman produced a large-scale map, and Tig was able to show them exactly where the wood was, with its clearings and dells. He gave them as well a good clear description of the gang of children. He was then told to stay there while they checked his story. He protested, but they were firm.

"And what if you do see them?" Tig objected morosely. "You might not recognise them, but I would. Anyway, if you want me to stay here, you'll have to lock me up."

"OK, OK," said Roberts eventually. "But mind you do what you're told."

Tig agreed, with mental reservations.

Heavy boots clumped through the undergrowth. Low voices cursed as brambles caught at clothes and faces. It occurred to Tig that if the gang were still there when he arrived, they must be either deaf or dead.

The clearing opened out before them, the dell with the hut. Further on they came to the smaller clearing which belonged to the stuffed stag. The bags and wallets still hung from its antlers.

Twenty-One

BACK in town, the police were busy. Radio-cars, enquiries in local areas, dogs, foot-patrols, searches of derelict buildings. Roberts had no time to consider smaller problems like Tig. His office at the station was turned into the centre of the operations.

Tig wandered about trying to avoid being noticed. He'd made a suggestion, which had been ignored. Be quiet, lad, he'd been told peremptorily. Just keep out of the way. So he had.

Later on, it occurred to Roberts that Tig could hardly spend the rest of the night sitting in a corner looking lost. It also came to him with something of a jolt that Tig's home was a cold and empty shell. How old was he? He looked younger than fourteen. Roberts took a quick glance at the boy, noted the dark-circled eyes, the general air of exhaustion.

"Got any friends, lad?"

Tig looked up, surprised.

"I mean, anyone who'd put you up for the night. Can't stay here. Neighbours down the road?"

"Sure," Tig said, unconcerned.

"Who? Name and address."

Tig was irritated. Same old thing. Give them half an inch, and they started organising you. He'd look after himself— he always had done.

"Come on, boy. Haven't got time to waste."

Tig got up and stretched.

"Pete's place. Pete Tyler. Silver Street. Number fifteen."

"That'll do. I'll get a car."

"I can walk."

"You'll do as you're told," Roberts snapped, his patience taut. "I want to know you get there."

"Have it your own way." Tig waited till the police-car came.

Pete's mother was welcoming and unfussy. She made up a bed for him on the sofa in the front room. Tig was tired, and he was grateful for not being bothered. Tomorrow was Saturday, so there was no need to play truant.

When morning came, grey and without hope, Roberts was again at his desk. Saturday morning. Over-cast, chance of rain. Crowds in the town for the week's shopping. Nobody at home to answer questions. Have you seen this child? A girl aged ten or eleven, long red hair, when last seen wearing faded jeans and dark blue sweater.

The papers would help. A big splash in the local evening rag might bring in useful information. Have to phone them. Get a reporter round.

Tig in the meantime had come bouncing back to life. After one of Pete's mother's breakfasts, he dragged Pete off into the town. He wouldn't tell him what he wanted, and Pete was full of injured complaints.

They found Liz at Rose's café. She looked surprised when Tig clapped her on the back and asked her where the boy-friend was.

"Which one?" Liz said.

"The reporter on the paper."

"Oh, him! He's not the only one. He's working. Why?"

"Big story down at the nick. Thought he might be interested."

Liz's eyes narrowed. "How do you know?"

Tig shrugged. "Where is he?"

"Might be anywhere. Is it important?"

"Could be. Still, you could pass it on to him, couldn't you?"

Liz considered. "I don't know . . ." she began.

"Aw, come on, Liz. I've got to be down there anyway."

Liz looked at him quickly. "Why?"

"Just have."

"All right. You need keeping an eye on."

Tig brightened. "Come on, then."

Liz looked worried and uncertain, but she came.

"Any news?" Tig asked.

"Not a thing. Sorry, son. Got any ideas?"

"Might have."

Steadman looked sharply at Tig and waited, but Tig stayed silent.

"Contrary little perisher, aren't you?" Steadman commented, but his voice was friendly. "I think you know a lot more than you've said. Why not get shot of it?"

"Nobody listens when I do," Tig said morosely.

"A chip on your shoulder does nothing except weigh you down, lad. I'm listening."

"You win," Tig said. "Where's the boss?"

"Inspector Roberts?"

"That's him."

"You've got something to say? The Inspector may be busy. I'll see."

Steadman tipped a wink at the sergeant behind the desk, who lifted his telephone and spoke quietly into the receiver.

"The Inspector will see you in his office," the sergeant announced.

"Let's go," Tig said. "You as well, Liz."

They all trooped up to Inspector Roberts's office. Tig was embarrassed now, and wished he hadn't started it.

Roberts faced them, his face lined and tired.

"John English wanted to tell you something, sir," said Steadman.

"Well?"

"This is Pete," Tig said. "And she's Liz Prior, my cousin."

He looked round. There they were, all standing in a row, like so many puppets waiting for their strings to be pulled. He'd have to go through with it now. He shambled over to the window and looked down at the heads of the people in the street.

"Well?" Roberts repeated.

"It's about the robbery," Tig began, talking to the glass in the window.

"Yes, yes, That's been dealt with. We've got them. There's something else now."

"I know," Tig growled. Why wouldn't they shut up for two minutes so that he could say what he had to say?

"This *is* about the robbery, though. That night in the alley, well, I saw two thieves, because they had a torch, and I recognised them next day. The two musicians. The one who was dressed up as a woman had some sort of scent. It was the same smell. It was them all right."

"We know that," Roberts said wearily.

Tig went on looking out of the window. He wished he was outside in the sharp sunshine which was now beginning to break through the tattered clouds. It was stuffy in this room.

"But there was someone else," Tig went on.

"The insider."

"Yes. Somebody pushed the bag through the window."

"You said you couldn't give a description."

"Well, I couldn't, could I? The light was all wrong. It was just a shape. I read about the coins and the exhibition in the paper. Somebody must've got into that room, pinched the coins, chucked the bag out of the window. Right?"

Roberts grunted.

"And you haven't got the third one yet, have you?"

"No," Roberts admitted reluctantly.

"Do you know who it is?"

"No." Roberts's irritation bubbled over into sarcasm. "But I suppose you do."

"Yes."

Roberts pushed his chair back. His face showed his disbelief.

"Go on," he said.

"It's complicated," Tig was apologetic. "It came to me all of a sudden. You know when I came in first, that night of the robbery, and a copper asked me my name? Well, I wasn't going to tell him that. Enough trouble already. So I told him it was French. The only thing I could think of that wasn't English, see?"

"We worked that out," Steadman said.

Tig glanced at him and then turned back to the window. "Well, *you* knew about this French and English business. And I'd told Pete, so Pete knew. But then that evening when we found out where their hide-out was — you remember, Pete? — and they came charging out when I chucked a stone, I heard them talking. It didn't mean anything at the time, but I remembered it afterwards. One of them said something about 'getting that French-English kid!' Something like that. Well, that was me. Point is, how did they know? It was my name, and, as well as that, the false one. How did they know?"

The question hung in the air. There was silence, broken by the scraping of Roberts's chair.

"Carry on," he said quietly.

"Well, you didn't tell them, did you? Nor did Pete. There was only one other person I told about it. In Rose's café. We'd gone there for some coffee. You were there, Pete. So was Liz."

Tig turned round slowly, his eyes fixed firmly on his toe-caps.

"Liz was the only other one who knew, so Liz must've told them."

Liz Prior laughed.

"Hey! Listen to that!" she said. "I saved you from them, don't you remember? In that shop."

"I remember. I couldn't think at the time why it all

seemed like a play. A put-up job, wasn't it? The thieves had to find out how much I knew, how much I'd seen. They'd seen me, hiding behind that lamp-post in the alley. They had to know whether I'd recognise them again. That was your job, wasn't it, Liz? You did it very well."

Liz had gone very white. "You can't pin it on me!"

Roberts looked up.

"Miss Prior, were you at the White Lion Hotel that night?"

"Yes, but —"

"I think a certain amount of explanation is required, Miss Prior. Perhaps if we brought you face to face with the two we've got —"

"They won't split. Digger would never —"

"Digger? The official names have been released, Miss Prior, but not the nicknames by which one of them is known to his associates."

Gradually Liz was forced to tell the truth. Yes, she knew the man with the black beard, she knew about the robberies; she had helped the two of them a good many times when an extra pair of hands was needed. It had often come in useful to pretend to be friendly with a reporter on the *Evening Herald*. Going around with him had given her the entry into a lot of places where she could use her eyes to advantage.

It was she who had passed the bag of coins out through the window of the White Lion, though the robbery itself had been done by Digger. He had left her with the bag while he and his pal had sauntered out through the front door and then round to the back, to the alley where Tig had seen them in the fog. The alley where old Bill was lying, hurt but still conscious, in the gutter.

She swore she'd had nothing to do with the beating up of Old Bill. That must have been Digger.

As she talked, trying to spin a tale which sounded better than it was, Tig kept his gaze fixed on the street. He didn't want to listen, but he couldn't help it.

After Liz, accompanied by Steadman, had gone, Tig said, "What about the girl with the red hair?"

"Still not found," Roberts said. "Thanks for the information. Can't have been easy."

" 'Sall right. Nobody mucks me about like that."

"Independent, eh?"

"Yep."

"All right, Tig. I'm asking for help. Where do you think that girl is?"

"There's one place I bet she'll go to."

"Where?"

"I'll take you there," Tig offered.

"You'll tell me," Roberts ordered.

Tig pushed his hands deeper into his pockets. "Coming Pete?"

"Sit down!" Roberts roared at him. "Why the hell don't you do what you're told?"

Tig stayed standing. Anger glistened in his eyes. The same old story. Why the hell don't you do what you're told? As though it was some sort of crime not to.

"I'll take you there," he repeated. He was tired of the whole thing. "I'll show you where the coins are too, if you still want them. They're in an iron box at the bottom of the bonfire on the common."

Roberts swallowed his pride. He ordered a car.

In the little clearing in the wood where the stuffed stag held court the bright sunlight streamed over red leaves and brown earth. The stag's fur was patchy, and the damage to its left foreleg was horribly clear.

On the wooden base of the stag, with her arms crooked round its legs, and her red hair spilling out in a tangled mass, lay the girl, all alone. She looked asleep.

But when Roberts went over to her, and picked her up, she screamed. She screamed all the time as they took her away.

"The Badden will get you!" she screamed, but nothing more.

Master of Morgana

ALLAN CAMPBELL McLEAN

'I stopped, panting, straining my ears for all they were worth. Above the loud thumping of my heart, I was certain I could hear the sound of hurrying feet scuffing the loose gravel on the road. I took to my heels. I was half-way down the road before I caught sight of him . . . Right away I knew he was my man.'

At that moment, sixteen year old Niall knew that his brother's near fatal fall was not a mere accident. Someone had fully intended Ruairidh to die when he fell deep into the gorge. But why should anyone want to rob quiet and solitary Ruairidh of his life? Move by move Niall is bound tighter in a web of intrigue and suspicion.

Set against the lonely, rugged background of the Isle of Skye, this is an immensely gripping adventure story for older readers.

The Hill of the Red Fox and *The Year of the Stranger* by Allan Campbell McLean are also in LIONS.

The Hill of the Red Fox

ALLAN CAMPBELL McLEAN

The newspaper headline read 'Unknown Man Found Shot'. Alasdair had run into the 'unknown man' on the train to Skye. In fact, the stranger had slipped him a last desperate message – 'Hunt at the Hill of the Red Fox MI5'.

There was soon no doubt in Alasdair's mind that his uncle, Murdo Beaton, was involved in the crime – and this time it wasn't a simple poaching operation – atomic scientists and their secrets were disappearing.

Who could Alasdair turn to? Duncan Mor was his only ally and *he* was on the run from the law. So he'd go to Major Cassell. But Alasdair had chosen badly . . .

'By the time I have finished this cigarette,' the Major announced, 'Alasdair Cameron will have ceased to bother anyone.'

The Year of the Stranger and *Master of Morgana*, more thrilling adventures for readers of ten and up, are also available in LIONS

Spellbinders in Suspense

ALFRED HITCHCOCK

Alfred Hitchcock has compiled a singularly gripping and spine-chilling collection of thirteen stories by some of the most powerful suspense writers around. Many of the stories, like Daphne du Maurier's *The Birds* and Richard Connell's *The Most Dangerous Game* chill you to the marrow; others, like Patrick Quentin's *Puzzle for Poppy* present a seemingly insoluble enigma; all have that unique ingredient to make your blood race with excitement.

For brave readers of twelve and up.

Monster Museum by Alfred Hitchcock is also available in Lions.

Alan Garner

THE WEIRDSTONE OF BRISINGAMEN
THE MOON OF GOMRATH
ELIDOR
THE OWL SERVICE

When Alan Garner's first book, *The Weirdstone of Brisingamen*, was published he was hailed by reviewers as a great new writer. *The Weirdstone* and its sequel *The Moon of Gomrath* are fantasies of striking imagination and power set around Alderley Edge in Cheshire where Alan Garner lives.

With the publication of *The Owl Service* Alan Garner received both the Guardian Award and the Carnegie Medal. Set in Wales, the story describes the reawakening of an ancient legend of jealousy and destruction which threatens to live again in Alison, Roger and Gwyn.

Alan Garner has been described in the *Times Educational Supplement* as 'one of the most exciting writers for young people today. He is producing work with strong plot structure, perceptive characterisation and vivid language. Furthermore, there is in his writing a basic integrity within which the poetic imagination may have free rein. It is a combination of qualities that creates literature that will be read and read again.'

The Third Class Genie

ROBERT LEESON

Disasters were leading two nil on Alec's disaster-triumph scorecard, when he slipped into the vacant factory lot, locally known as the Tank. Ginger Wallace was hot on his heels, ready to destroy him, and Alec had escaped just in the nick of time. There were disasters awaiting him at home too, when he discovered that he would have to move out of his room and into the boxroom. And, of course, there was school . . .

But Alec's luck changed when he found a beer can that was still sealed, but obviously empty. Stranger still, when he held it up to his ear, he could hear a faint snoring . . . When Alec finally opened the mysterious can, something happened that gave triumphs a roaring and most unexpected lead.

A hilarious story for readers of ten upwards.

When Hitler Stole Pink Rabbit

JUDITH KERR

Anna was only nine in 1933, too busy with her school work and her friends to take much notice of the posters of Adolf Hitler and the menacing swastikas plastered over Berlin. Being Jewish, she thought, was just something you were because your parents and grandparents were Jewish. Suddenly Anna's father was unaccountably and frighteningly missing. Shortly after, she and her brother were hurried out of Germany by their mother with alarming secrecy. Then began their rootless, wandering existence as refugees. Their life was often difficult and sad, but Anna soon discovered that all that really mattered was that the family was together.

An outstanding book for readers of ten upwards.